GIANT
CARGO PLANES

Nicholas A. Veronico and Jim Dunn

MBI Publishing Company

For Betty.
For 1st Sgt. James P. Dunn, US Army Infantry, 38th Infantry Division, WWII.

First published in 1999 by MBI Publishing Company, 729 Prospect Avenue, PO Box 1, Osceola, WI 54020-0001 USA

MBI Publishing Company books are also available at discounts in bulk quantity for industrial or sales-promotional use. For details write to Special Sales Manager at Motorbooks International Wholesalers & Distributors, 729 Prospect Avenue, Osceola, WI 54020-0001 USA.

Library of Congress Cataloging-in-Publication Data Available

ISBN 0-7603-0510-2

On the front cover: C-5B, serial number 84-0060, from the 21st Airlift Squadron at Travis AFB is about to be refueled at 21,000 feet off the Mendocino Coast of Northern California. *Fred 07* will make a number of connections with *Quest 52,* a KC-10 from the 70th Air Refueling Squadron (ARS), also based at Travis, to requalify several pilots for aerial refueling. *Jim Dunn*

On the frontispiece: The pressurized lower cargo compartment of the Galaxy has a total usable volume of 34,796 cubic feet. It measures 19 feet wide by 121 feet long, with heights ranging from 9 feet 6 inches beneath the wing to 13 feet 6 inches in the aft section. It can carry an M1 Abrams main battle tank, as well as a CH-47 Chinook helicopter, and in extreme cases, 290 troopers on palletized seat rows. *Jim Dunn*

On the title page: While C-5B, 86-0021, returns from a 1998 Airlift Rodeo mission C-17A, 95-0105 arrives with Gen. Walter Kross, commander of the Air Mobility Command (AMC). Gen. Kross has stated that it would be too expensive to replace the C-5 with a smaller aircraft, such as the C-17, because of the large numbers that would be required to perform the missions. *Jim Dunn*

On the back cover: At the current procurement rate of 13 aircraft per year, the 120th and last C-17 in the initial order will be completed by 2005. Many believe that the U.S. Air Force will need at least twice this number of Globemaster IIIs just to maintain its strategic airlift capabilities at present levels. *Jim Dunn*

Designed by Rebecca Allen

Printed in Hong Kong

Contents

Acknowledgments   7

1   The Evolution of Airlift Planes   8

2   Logistics Transport System 476L
Lockheed's C-141 Starlifter   20

3   Giant of the Airways
Lockheed's C-5 Galaxy   36

4   KC-10A Extender
Airlifter and Aerial Refueler   50

5   C-17 Globemaster III
High-Tech Cargo Carrier   64

6   Giant Soviet Cargo Planes   82

7   The Future of Airlifters   92

Index   96

Acknowledgments

The authors would like to thank the Active Duty, Air Force Reserve, and Air National Guard personnel of the U.S. Air Force's Air Mobility Command (AMC). We would also like to thank the public affairs officers of AMC and of the Airlift Rodeo for their assistance. Thanks to the manufacturers: from Boeing, George Sillia, Ron Henderson Jr., Richard L. Fuller, and Don Hansen; and from Lockheed, Doug E. Oliver. Special thanks to Major Tom Dolney, Captain Tatianna Stead, Capt. Craig Heighton, Capt. Tania Daniels, and Chuck Jones for making many of our flights and base visits for this book a success.

This book would not be as complete without the contributions of many of our colleagues. Thanks to Jean Bizot, Roger Cain, Ed Davies, Greg Davis, Mark Dentone, Robert F. Dorr, Wayne McPherson Gomes, A. Kevin Grantham, Michael Gruenenfelder, Todd Hackbarth, Earl Holmquist, Jack Lambert, William T. Larkins, Gary Leiser, Gerald Liang, Terry M. Love, Toyokazu Matsuzaki, Thomas Wm. McGarry, Dan O'Hara, Milo Peltzer, Carl E. Porter, Jon Proctor, Wayne Saunders, Doug Scroggins, Ron Strong, Kim Tamez, Scott Thompson, Dan F. Webb, and the late Emil Strasser. A special thanks to Rene J. Francillon for his support and guidance in this effort, and our editors at MBI Publishing, Michael Haenggi and Christopher Batio.

Nicholas A. Veronico
San Carlos, California

Jim Dunn
Sacramento, California

Staging equipment and support vehicles are loaded aboard C-17 (85-0106), The Spirit of Bob Hope, at the start of a 25-day European tour by the U.S. Air Force Band. They performed for military personnel on duty in Hungary, Croatia, Bosnia, Italy, Macedonia, Germany and the United Kingdom. *Boeing*

1 The Evolution of Airlift Planes

ifteen years after the Wright brothers took to the skies over Kitty Hawk, North Carolina, the world had come to realize the potential of the airplane as a weapon. Single seat S.P.A.D. and Fokker biplanes had bloodied the skies over Germany and France while Caproni, Gotha, and Handley Page biplane bombers took the war to the cities and industrial centers of Europe. These biplanes could lift only a small useful load, rarely more than the crew, some small bombs, and the gasoline needed to power the aircraft.

In the years following "The Great War," attentions turned to expanding commerce and increasing the speed with which mail was delivered. By the mid-1920s, the days of fabric-covered wooden fuselages were gone, and a new generation of welded steel-tube fuselage aircraft with metal skin, such as the Ford Tri-Motor, were being introduced. Air/rail travel from coast to coast began in mid-1929. It was now possible to travel in comfort from New York to Los Angeles. Passengers journeyed by train at night—sleeping in Pullman cars—and flew during daylight hours. Thus, a trip from New York to Los Angeles could be accomplished in two days and two nights. The biggest drawback was that the Tri-Motors could only accommodate 10 passengers and very little luggage. Nevertheless, payloads were improving, and that's where the airlines would make their money.

By the late 1920s, three fledgling aircraft manufacturers who would later dominate the industry—

Douglas sold hundreds of DC-3s to the airlines prior to World War II. When America became involved in the conflict, most airliners were impressed into military service. Designated the C-47 Skytrain in Army Air Corps service, more than 10,000 were purchased for military use. This aircraft was built as a C-41 VIP transport and assigned serial number 38-502 and was often used by Gen. H.H. "Hap" Arnold. It is currently owned by the Otis Spunkmeyer Co., and is used for aerial tours of the San Francisco Bay area. *Nicholas A. Veronico*

Boeing, Douglas, and Lockheed—were in various stages of expansion. Boeing had made a name for itself building fighters, scout planes, and its 12-passenger, tri-motor Model 80. The Douglas Company was formed in July 1921, and gained fame for its single-engine biplane World Cruisers that circumnavigated the globe in 1924. The Loughead brothers, Allan and Malcolm, built their first airplane in 1913. After forming the Loughead Aircraft Company, they changed its name to the phonetic spelling, "Lock-heed," built the Vega and Orion monoplanes, and by the mid-1930s were selling the 10-passenger Model 10 Electra.

By February 1933, Boeing had flown its revolutionary 10-passenger Model 247 which featured all-metal construction, a low wing, and twin 550-horsepower Pratt & Whitney Wasp S1D1 engines. The 247 could carry 10 passengers, their

When Douglas began to deliver C-54 Skymasters to the Army in March 1942, they were painted in the standard Olive Drab (OD) finish. This included C-54A 42-107451 that was built specially for President Franklin D. Roosevelt. Named *Sacred Cow*, it had conference and staterooms, plus an electric lift for the president's wheelchair. Wearing OD for the first time, C-54D 42-72449 arrives at McClellan AFB, California, for display at the base's museum. *Jim Dunn*

luggage, and 400 pounds of mail for a distance of 485 miles. One year later, Douglas flew its larger, faster DC-2. Fully loaded, it was capable of flying 1,000 miles with a crew of two plus 14 passengers and their luggage.

The introduction of large flying boats, Martin's M-130 in December 1934 and Boeing's 314 in June 1938, began to give aircraft even larger cargo-carrying capabilities. The flying boat's large payload, when compared to its contemporaries, brought interest from both military and commercial interests.

Pushing the envelope of aircraft design one step further and following on the success of its DC-2 and the DC-3, Douglas began flight testing a four-engine, tricycle-landing-gear transport known as the DC-4E. This aircraft first flew on June 7, 1938, and was extensively tested and demonstrated. Realizing that the concept was sound but needed refinement, American Airlines, Eastern Airlines, and United Airlines all signed up to buy a newly redesigned DC-4. It was powered by four 1,450-horsepower Pratt & Whitney R-2000 radial engines and was capable of carrying a 22,000 pound payload for 2,000 miles. Orders for 61 aircraft had been received before America was drawn into World War II.

The demands of global warfare pushed aircraft designers farther. At the outbreak of hostilities, the U.S. Army Air Corps was forced to rely on converted bomber-type aircraft to move its cargo by air. The mighty B-17 Flying Fortress and B-24 Liberator were stripped of armament and converted to freighters or troop transports to carry supplies and men to far-ranging battle fronts. They were the only aircraft capable of lifting a large load over a long distance. In the struggle to move materiel, Douglas' commercial DC-3 was impressed into military service and, when built new for the Army Air Forces, was redesignated as the C-47 Skytrain. Its airline-style seats were removed, the floor was strengthened, and the normal airstair door was replaced

An extension of the C-54 program was Douglas Aircraft's C-118 (commercial DC-6). The C-118 featured a lengthened, pressurized fuselage and more powerful 2,100 horsepower R-2800 radial engines. This gave the C-118 the capacity to haul 27,000 pounds of cargo or 74 fully laden troops. C-118A, serial number 53-3295, rests at Los Angeles International Airport in 1959. *E.A. Strasser*

by a wide, two-panel cargo door large enough to drive a jeep through.

While America and the Allies built-up their air arms, Germany and the Axis powers had been demonstrating the capabilities of cargo aircraft used in the air assault role. During the opening days of the Spanish Civil War, German-built Junkers Ju-52 transports made 461 flights airlifting 7,350 of Franco's Nationalist troops and their equipment from Africa to Spain during July and August 1936. Airlift proved a decisive factor—if the troops had traveled to Spain by ship, they could have been intercepted by the Spanish Republican Navy. In the following month, Ju-52s flew 324 sorties carrying 5,455 troops, and in October, 1,157 additional troops were delivered on 83 flights.

When Adolf Hitler's Nazi army marched into Austria in March 1938, the first airlift operation of what would become World War II took place. A paratroop battalion was delivered by Ju-52/3s from Germany to Graz-Thalerhof, Austria. During

1940, Hitler's forces undertook three major airlift operations. On April 9, Operation Weserübung—the invasion of Norway—employed more than 570 Ju-52/3s, which moved 29,280 troops, 2,376 tons of cargo, and 259,300 gallons of gasoline. On May 10, the invasion of the Low Countries saw 430 Ju-52/3s drop paratroops and carry supplies. And in November, German Ju-52s airlifted men and supplies from Foggia, Italy, to Tirana, Albania, in support of the Italian Army. During this 50-day reinforcement, 4,028 sorties were flown carrying 30,000 soldiers and 4,700 tons of equipment and supplies.

To support its widely deployed armies, German aeronautical engineers developed a number of other airlifters, including the four-engine Focke-Wulf Fw-200 Condor and the Arado Ar-232, and the giants of its airlifter fleet, the Messerschmitt Me-321 Gigant transport glider and its six-engine powered Me-323 variant. The Me-321's maximum loaded weight was 75,840 pounds and the Me-323 version could lift off weighing 99,210 pounds. The aircraft featured large clam-shell nose doors capable of accommodating trucks and other light vehicles as well as fully-loaded troops.

Germany's last major air assault came on May 20, 1941, when the Luftwaffe attempted an airborne invasion of the island of Crete. More than 10,000 men were to parachute onto Crete from 493 Ju-52/3s followed by an additional 750 men in 80 gliders. These troops were to establish landing fields where another 5,000 men would be landed, as well as enough supplies to sustain the invasion. Drought conditions had turned the island into a floating dust bowl. When the Ju-52/3s landed, they

Air National Guard units received C-124s in January 1966. In all, 10 ANG squadrons in seven different states flew the type until its final phase out in September 1974. Two Georgia ANG units, the 128th and 158th Military Airlift Squadrons, respectively, were the first unit to gain the C-124 and the last Air Force units to fly them. *Jim Dunn*

13

threw up tremendous dust clouds obscuring the airfields and paratroop landing zones. The island's British and Greek defenders were able to repel the landing and, in the process, destroy 271 German transports. Never again would the Germans mount such an ambitious airborne assault.

Meanwhile, America and her allies were faced with fighting a war on numerous fronts where the enemy held either air-, ground-, or sea-superiority, or a combination thereof. In the South Pacific, the Japanese held the islands, controlled the sea lanes, and maintained air superiority. Douglas' C-47 and C-54, the military version of its commercial DC-4, were used to transport troops from the mainland to staging bases in Hawaii and Australia. The Curtiss C-46 Commando, a twin-engine tail dragger larger than the C-47, is commonly associated with operations in the CBI (China-Burma-India) theater flying supplies from India, over the Himalayas to China.

America's first air assault operation in the South West Pacific began on September 5, 1943,

when 82 Fifth Air Force C-47s dropped paratroops to capture Nadzab Air Field in New Guinea. Four days later, the Fifth Army under General Mark Clark made an amphibious landing at Salerno while British paratroops landed on the Italian mainland. Operation Slapstick captured the naval base at Taranto.

By far, the bloodiest Allied air assault was the June 6, 1944, D-Day invasion of France when more than 1,400 C-47s and C-53s (paratrooper variants of the C-47) dropped three airborne divisions to secure the areas behind the invasion beachheads. Other operations included the invasion of southern France—Operation Dragoon—which saw the 1st Airborne Task Force dropped southwest of Cannes on August 15, 1944, to secure the rear areas of the beachhead. Simultaneously, three divisions of the U.S. VI Corps landed between Nice and Toulon, France. Operation Market-Garden began on September 17, 1944, with 1,546 troop transports and 478 gliders landing the U.S. 82nd and 101st Airborne and British 1st Airborne divisions in the Low Countries to secure bridgeheads across the Maas, Waal, and Neder-Rhine rivers. The final major airborne operation of the war, Operation Varsity, began on March 24, 1945, and saw more than 2,000 transports and gliders transport the U.S. 17th Airborne Division and British 6th Airborne Division into the heart of Nazi Germany.

Allied air assault operations and the need to transport cargo huge distances helped drive the future of airlift aircraft. During the years immediately prior to and following the cessation of hostilities, numerous cargo aircraft designs were developed and purchased by America and other countries.

Built for the planned invasion of Japan and introduced too late to see service in World War II, Fairchild's C-82 Packet was a giant step forward in cargo aircraft design—one that incorporated all of the cargo handling lessons learned in World War II into one aircraft. Many of the C-82's

The newest model of the Hercules is the C-130J. Its most distinctive feature is its scimitar-shaped six-bladed propellers. *Jim Dunn*

Lockheed's Constellation was designed to meet a 1939 airliner specification for Trans World Airlines. Only 22 aircraft reached the Army Air Forces before the end of World War II, but the type was later destined to see extensive service with the U.S. military. Despite its speed, the Constellation's major drawback was its high fuselage that required extensive ground handling equipment to load and unload heavy equipment. *Robert F. Dorr Collection*

features have been continued into today's giant cargo planes. The first C-82 flew its maiden flight on September 20, 1944, and a total of 220 were built. The Fairchild design featured twin 2,100-horsepower R-2800 radial engines, tricycle landing gear, a passenger loading door at the left front of the fuselage, and rear clam-shell loading doors under a high tail, enabling vehicles to easily access the airplane's interior. Production of the C-82 was discontinued in 1948 in favor of Fairchild's larger and more powerful C-119 Flying Boxcar, which was powered by Pratt & Whitney's 28-cylinder 3,250-horsepower R-4360 radial engines. C-119s were used extensively in Korea and Vietnam.

Also delivered too late to see service during the war years was Douglas' C-74 Globemaster I, powered by four 3,000-horsepower Pratt & Whitney R-4360-27 radial engines. The Globemaster I could carry 125 fully loaded troops, or 115 stretchers with medical staff, or 48,150 pounds of cargo over a maximum range of 7,250 miles. The type made its first flight on September 5, 1945, and production was canceled nine days later with the end of the war. Only 14 aircraft were completed.

Based upon Boeing's World War II B-29 and B-50 Superfortress, the C-97 Stratocruiser retained the same wings, empennage, and lower fuselage with a larger and wider upper fuselage, known as the "double bubble." Capable of flying at 30,000 feet, C-97s were able to cruise at 383 miles per hour while carrying a 20,000-pound load more than 3,000 miles. Later subtypes of the C-97 included the tanker variant, the KC-97, which served until final phase out in 1977.

Another transport concept based upon a bomber was Convair's XC-99, the transport version of its mammoth B-36 intercontinental bomber. Retaining the B-36's powerplant arrangement of six 3,000-horsepower R-4360 radial engines, the bomber's cavernous fuselage was stripped of armament and fitted with double decks, the upper for troops, and lower for cargo and vehicles. Although it reached the prototype stage, the C-99 was not acquired by the Air Force.

In the first major hostile act of the Cold War, Soviet Russia attempted to strangle the Allied-occupied sector in West Berlin by halting rail traffic into the city on June 11, 1948, and then blocking all surface communications on June 24.

First flown in 1947, Fairchild's C-119 Flying Boxcar was an outstanding improvement over World War II's impressed airliners. This purpose-built airlifter featured clam shell rear doors capable of handling many outsize loads, and could accommodate roll-on cargo. Flying Boxcars saw extensive service in Korea and Vietnam. *Robert F. Dorr Collection*

Two days later, the Berlin Airlift began. American and British Douglas C-47s were the first aircraft into the city. Berlin was under blockade for nearly one year, until the Russians finally backed down on May 12, 1949. Nearly 225 cargo planes flew 277,569 sorties in support of the Berlin Airlift delivering 536,705 tons of food; 1,586,028 tons of coal; and 202,775 tons of additional supplies including bulldozers and construction equipment, aviation fuel, aircraft engines and spare parts, as well as mail, and pierced steel planking (PSP) for runways—everything a city and airport would need to survive.

From its short-lived C-74, Douglas took the wings, engines, and tail surfaces and matched them with a new, larger fuselage to produce the C-124 Globemaster II. Clam-shell doors were incorporated under the flight deck ahead of the nose landing gear to enable vehicles to roll on or off of the lower deck. An upper deck was used for passenger seating and light cargo, and the C-124 featured a mid-fuselage elevator that dropped to ground level. Globemaster IIs could carry most of the U.S. Army's large cargo, and were capable of hauling 50,000 pounds for 2,300 miles. That translated into space for 200 fully-equipped troops, or 123 stretcher patients plus 45 soldiers and 15 doctors and nurses. The prototype C-124 first flew on November 27, 1949, and the aircraft served until 1974.

After the Korean Conflict, there was an escalation of the Cold War. The perfection of Intercontinental Ballistic Missiles (ICBMs) capable of unmanned delivery of nuclear weapons struck fear in our nation's heart. Construction of hardened missile silos across the country required new airlifters capable of moving construction materials and missiles to remote locations. Construction of the Arctic Distant Early Warning (DEW) Line also required larger, more capable

The Douglas C-133A Cargomaster was designed to handle large, oversize loads and could carry 96 percent of the U.S. Army's vehicles. The plane featured a built-in rear loading ramp and an upward-hinged cargo door in the left front fuselage. Cargomasters played a significant role in establishing the U.S. Air Force's ICBM force by transporting Convair-built Atlas ICBMs from the factory in San Diego, California, to various Strategic Air Command bases. The 34th C-133A built, serial number 57-1614, unloads an Atlas ICBM at Francis E. Warren AFB, Wyoming. *Robert F. Dorr Collection*

The most widely recognized cargo-carrying aircraft in the U.S. Air Force is the Boeing-built C-135 Stratolifter and its tanker variant the KC-135 Stratotanker, both similar in external appearance to Boeing's commercial 707 airliner. The Stratolifter is capable of carrying 126 troops in removable seat modules, or 80 passengers in the tanker configuration. More than 40 different subtypes of the C-135 have been operated by the U.S. and foreign armed forces. Military variants of the C/KC-135 series will fly with the U.S. Air Force well into the 21st Century.

The most ubiquitous cargo plane is Lockheed's legendary C-130 Hercules. The prototype Hercules was flown on August 23, 1954. The C-130's primary role is the transportation of cargo and its 3,820-mile range coupled with its ability to haul a 35,700-pound payload and to land on short,

aircraft. Douglas' C-133 Cargomaster was the answer to the Army and Air Force's need for a strategic airlifter and truly met the 1950's definition of a "giant cargo plane." A long fuselage, tall tail, and high wing carrying four Pratt & Whitney T34-P-3 turboprop engines gave the C-133 a sleek look. The first Cargomaster flew on April 23, 1956, giving the Air Force the capability to deliver 110,000 pounds by air, including its Atlas, Thor, and Jupiter missiles. Oversize cargo was loaded through rear clam-shell doors and a standard cargo door was fitted in the left front fuselage. The normal load for a C-133A was 42,000 pounds delivered up to 4,000 miles from the airport of origin. A total of 50 C-133s were built in both "A" and T34-P-9W powered "B" models. Cargomasters served until 1971 when they were replaced by the jet-powered Lockheed C-5 Galaxy.

Boeing's C-97 was the first transport aircraft built after the end of World War II. Based on the B-29 bomber's wings, landing gear, and tail, the Stratocruiser was the first airlifter to feature double-deck flooring that enabled cargo to be carried below the main deck which could be filled with troops or vehicles. Later variants included the KC-97, shown here, fitted with an aerial refueling boom. *Robert F. Dorr Collection*

unimproved airstrips has made it the choice of the U.S. military and 60 other nations. C-130s are often seen on the nightly news bringing humanitarian aid to impoverished nations or those struck by natural disasters, most recently Haiti, Bosnia, Somalia, and Rwanda. Three primary models, the "A," "B," and "E," proceeded the most numerous subtype, the C-130H. It is powered by four 5,910-horsepower Allison T-56A-15 prop jet engines, has upgraded avionics, and redesigned outer wing panels. More than 350 C-130Hs were acquired by the United States before the line was shut down in the early 1990s. The U.S. military plans to upgrade its fleet of Hercules transports by acquiring the new C-130J powered by four Allison AE 2100D3 6,000 shaft-horsepower engines turning all-composite Dowty R391 propellers. The "J" model's flight deck is designed for two-crew person operation, has digital avionics, and mission specific computers among other upgrades. The C-130J can carry vehicles, 92 troops, or 64 paratroopers, or 74 stretcher patients and attendants, or 54 passengers on palletized seat modules, or up to five 463L freight pallets, or any combination for a payload of

Lockheed's C-130 Hercules is a tactical airlifter capable of carrying 42,637 pounds of cargo or up to 92 passengers. Its versatility, reliability, and range have made it a desirable aircraft for air forces the world over. Many aircraft have been modified to fill other roles including command and control, electronic countermeasures, search and rescue. One of the most interesting variants is the AC-130H Spectre gunship shown here. It carries two 20mm Vulcan cannons, one 40mm Bofors cannon, and one 105mm howitzer to suppress air defenses and support ground troops. *U.S. Air Force*

18

Boeing's C-135 and KC-135 tanker/transport was the first all-jet transport in the Air Force's inventory. A total of 732 KC-135s were built under six major designations. In addition to hauling cargo, the KC-135A has a total fuel capacity of 31,200 gallons carried in wing and fuselage tanks that can be off-loaded when performing in the aerial refueling role. This Utah ANG KC-135E orbits above the English Channel awaiting thirsty F-111s from RAF Upper Heyford on March 27, 1987. *Ssgt. Fernando Serna via Dorr*

41,790 pounds. With a payload of 40,000 pounds, the C-130J has a range of 3,262 miles.

The evolution of airlift aircraft has taken nearly 70 years—from the C-47 Skytrain to the tactical C-130J Hercules. Many large aircraft were built during and after the World War II years, and four models stand out from the rest: Lockheed's C-141 Starlifter and C-5 Galaxy, McDonnell Douglas' KC-10 Extender, and Boeing's C-17 Globemaster III.

2 Logistics Transport System 476L
Lockheed's C-141 Starlifter

The first all-jet powered airlift plane was Lockheed's C-141 Starlifter. Envisioned during the mid- to late-1950s at a time when Boeing had introduced its all-jet B-52 Stratofortress bomber and C-135 Stratolifter transport, the Military Air Transport Service (MATS) required an aircraft capable of handling both personnel and the Army's heavy, outsized equipment. At the time, the majority of MATS operations were being flown with converted airliners such as the C-118/DC-6 and C-121/Lockheed 1049 Constellation—neither capable of handling roll-on, roll-off cargo. The few Fairchild C-119s, C-123s, and Douglas C-124s and C-133s that were in the inventory were inadequate to handle the Army, Navy, and Air Force's combined volume of cargo. The Army believed that to combat hostile threats, its airlift requirement called for the rapid deployment of nearly four divisions to any location in the world. Each division would need 5,000 tons of equipment if landed at an established military base, or 11,000 tons if deployed to an open area. In the mid-1950s, it would have taken 272 C-133 loads to move 5,000 tons. When you consider that only 50 of the type were built, moving 5,000 tons was a formidable task.

Development of the medium-range aircraft that would become the Starlifter began in 1959 when the Air Force sought research and development funding for an all-jet cargo transport. The proposed aircraft was to be capable of strategic and tactical airlift, have the ability to air-drop

Starlifters were delivered to the Military Air Transport Service in a bare metal finish beginning in October 1964. Photographed in May 1965, C-141A, 63-8088, was the 19th Starlifter built and the first to be based with the 1501st Air Transport Wing at Travis AFB, California. *Golden Bear* spent nearly all its career at Travis and is now retired there, awaiting display in a place of honor on the base. *Nicholas A. Veronico Collection*

The first Starlifter built was one of four aircraft never given the C-141B modification. Number 61-2775 first flew on December 17, 1963, and spent much of its 34 years with the USAF at Edwards AFB. Seen here departing Yokota AB, Japan, in January 1991, it logged just over 9,000 hours before it was retired for display at Dover AFB in February 1998. *Toyokazu Matsuzaki*

men and supplies, and be able to operate at low altitudes. Department of Defense (DoD) planners reviewed the Army's airlift requirements and established that a future airlifter should be able to carry a maximum load of 60,000 pounds over more than 3,500 nautical miles.

The request for proposals for Logistics Transport System 476L were sent to the aerospace industry in December 1960. The competition was fierce between Lockheed, Douglas, Boeing, and Convair, but on March 13, 1961, it was announced that Lockheed had prevailed. Its design, designated the C-141A Starlifter, first rolled off the company's Marietta, Georgia, assembly line in August 1963, and flew for the first time four months later on December 17, 1963. The new Starlifter sat low to the ground, had a shoulder-mounted wing spanning nearly 160 feet, a T-tail, and clam-shell rear doors that incorporated a loading ramp. The "A" model's fuselage cross section is 10 feet, 4 inches wide by 9 feet 1.25 inches tall, and its cargo compartment

is 70 feet long giving a useable volume of 6,530.5 cubic feet. The prototype was polished metal, and although it could not handle the volume of cargo that its piston-engine contemporaries like the C-124 could, its speed was nearly 200 miles per hour faster, thereby increasing its productivity.

C-141As entered service with the Military Air Transport Service (MATS) in April 1965, with the last of the 284 aircraft ordered by the military being delivered in February 1968. One additional aircraft was built for demonstration to possible commercial customers, and was later sold to NASA. The plane, registered N714NA, was fitted with a 36-inch telescope installed in the port upper fuselage, forward of the wing and behind the cockpit, and operated as the Kuiper Flying Observatory. One aircraft, serial number 61-2777, was extensively modified as an Advanced Radar Test-Bed (ARTB) and was redesignated an NC-141. This and three other aircraft did not receive the "B" model upgrade. A number of C-141As were also modified to transport an 86,207-pound LGM-30 Minuteman ICBM.

Table I—C-141B Specifications

Length:	168 feet, 3.5 inches
Wing Span:	159 feet, 11 inches
Height:	39 feet, 3 inches
Empty Weight:	153,350 pounds
Maximum Weight:	323,000 pounds
Operating Weight:	150,000 pounds of cargo or 160,781 pounds of troops
Maximum Cabin Load:	68,725 pounds
Maximum Cruising Speed:	566 miles per hour
Unrefueled Range with Max Payload:	2,170 miles
Powerplants:	Four Pratt & Whitney TF33-P-7 turbofan engines rated at 21,000 pounds thrust each
Speed:	425 miles per hour
Crew:	Five
Cargo Capacity:	Thirteen 463L pallets which are 104 inches by 94 inches, or 200 fully equipped troops, or 155 paratroopers, or 103 litter patients plus attendants, or a combination including vehicles

The major modification that created the first C-141B in 1977 brought about a significant improvement in the capabilities of the Starlifter. Two fuselage plugs extended its length by 23 feet 4 inches and increased usable volume by nearly 75 percent. While maximum payload went from 70,847 pounds to 90,880 pounds, it was the addition of in-flight refueling that has paid dividends for the Air Force. *Carl E. Porter*

Starlifters were the first jet transports to be used in airborne operations. The C-141B can be configured to carry 200 troops or 155 fully-equipped paratroopers in canvas side-facing seats. In October 1983 during Operation Urgent Fury, C-141s from the 63rd MAW deployed paratroopers in a low-altitude assault on Grenada. Six years later, the largest airborne assault since World War II occurred during Operation Just Cause in Panama. *Jim Dunn*

The Starlifter's first practical demonstration was during Operation Blue Light in December 1965 and January 1966. During Blue Light, a total of 231 sorties were flown, moving 2,952 troops and 4,749 tons of cargo from Hickam Air Force Base, Hawaii, to Pleiku, Vietnam. Eighty-eight of the sorties were flown by Starlifters, which accomplished each mission 70 percent faster than piston-powered C-124s or turboprop-powered C-133s.

It wasn't until long after the end of the Vietnam War that Starlifters were given a camouflage paint scheme. In fact, this more military look wasn't applied until after the C-141B modifications were completed. With the new look came an unofficial new nickname. The Starlifter was now the "Star Lizard," and aircrews found themselves with one hot airplane. Sitting on the ramp, the dark exterior paint scheme greatly increased the interior temperature. *Jim Dunn*

To further demonstrate the quantum leap the C-141 provided to U.S. airlift capabilities, in November and December 1967, Operation Eagle Thrust saw the deployment of nearly the entire 101st Airborne Division (10,024 personnel) and 5,357 tons of equipment from Kentucky to Vietnam. Each one-way trip covered almost 10,000 miles, and the movement was accomplished in 391 sorties of which Starlifters flew 369. Turboprop-powered C-133s flew the trip in 100 hours, having to make numerous stops en route. C-141s covered the distance in less than 30 hours.

During the course of the war, thousands of C-141 missions were flown to and from Vietnam. Starlifters brought the tools of war directly from the states to the theater of operations and, sadly, returned with a planeload of casualties.

Military Airlift Command (MAC) was faced with a new challenge on January 27, 1973, when the Vietnamese cease-fire began. American troops, equipment, dependents, and numerous Vietnamese nationals had to be brought home. In conjunction with aircraft from commercial airlines, MAC began Operation Countdown to move these

Despite its age, when the "go" was given for the start of Operation Desert Shield, the first USAF aircraft into Saudi Arabia was a C-141B from the 437th MAW, Charleston AFB, South Carolina. Of the 15,800 airlift support missions during the Gulf War, Starlifters flew 7,047 of them, transporting more than 41,400 passengers and 139,600 tons of cargo. *Rene J. Francillon*

The last of 285 Starlifters built by Lockheed was 67-0166, which was delivered to the USAF in February 1968. Due to its many years in the command support mission, by 1997 it had only 18,033 hours, about 10,000 hours fewer than any other C-141B. High-time C-141B is 65-0259 with 43,087 hours. *Jim Dunn*

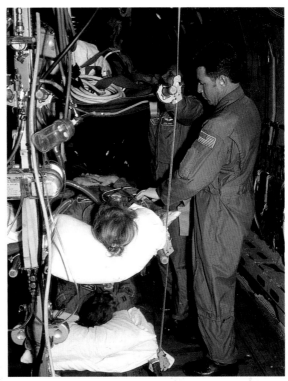

During a July 1998 flight, members of the 349th Aeromedical Evacuation Squadron from Travis AFB conduct a training exercise to maintain their proficiency and qualify new crews. Each member must fly at least one mission every 60 days to stay current. Air Force Reserve and Air National Guard crews make up 95 percent of USAF aeromedical evacuation personnel. *Jim Dunn*

people and materiel. The operation lasted from January 29 to March 29, 1973.

While evacuating Americans and South Vietnamese from the war-torn nation, two other important missions took place—Operations Homecoming and Babylift. On February 12, 1973, two C-130s flew support teams to Hanoi to prepare for the arrival of three C-141s to begin Operation Homecoming, the repatriation of American prisoners of war (POWs). Major James E. Marrott and his co-pilot John J. Shinoskie of the 63rd Military Airlift Wing flew C-141A 66-0177. They were the first Starlifter crew to repatriate American POWs from Hanoi to Clark Air Base, Philippines, and then on to Travis Air Force Base, California. In all, 591 American POWs returned home, most aboard Starlifters. Many airlifter crews reported that Operation Homecoming was the most satisfying mission they had ever flown. In April 1975 Operation Babylift involved the movement of 1,794 Southeast Asian orphans to the United States. C-141s carried 949 of those children.

While C-141 crews were busy in the Vietnam theater, additional crews were being called to airlift supplies and equipment to an allied nation half a world away. On October 6, 1973, during the Jewish holy day of Yom Kippur, the Egyptian Army launched an attack against Israel across the Suez Canal. In support of Israel, the United States initiated Operation Nickel Grass to supply materiel to the Middle Eastern nation. Many European countries denied landing rights to the U.S. airlifters, which brought the C-141's lack of aerial refueling capabilities to the forefront. Despite this drawback, C-141As flew 421 sorties delivering more than 10,000 tons of combat equipment in 30 days.

continued on page 32

Demonstrating Skills at AMC's Airlift Rodeo

The community of military airlifters rarely gets the attention that some other military fliers do. Except for the Berlin Airlift of 50 years ago, few airlift missions have ever attracted much coverage from the media. Today, do we remember the months of backbreaking work done by airlifters to support Desert Shield, or the 40 days of Operation Desert Storm?

For many years, airlifters did not even have a competitive event in which to showcase their ability to perform these missions. While the Strategic Air Command (SAC) had its bombing competitions and the Tactical Air Command (TAC) had the famous William Tell and Gunsmoke gunnery meets, the crews of the Military Airlift Command (MAC) went about the daily business of supporting not only SAC and TAC,

but also organizations like the Red Cross and United Nations.

When MAC planners finally got around to creating a competitive event for its crews, they designed it to emphasize the teamwork needed to perform the airlift mission. Named Volant Rodeo, this would be a competition for teams rather than individuals. If a unit were to win the title of "World's Best Airlifters," it would take the combined talents of many working in several different fields to achieve it.

This Rodeo was to be an annual competition with events for aircrew, aerial port, maintenance, combat control, and combat security personnel. It would be open to teams from all branches of service, including those in the Reserves and Air National Guard.

With Mt. Rainier in the background, the French team competes in the Engine Running On/Offload (ERO) event at the 1994 Airlift Rodeo. The French and German teams are the only ones that use the twin-engine Transall C-160 in the competition. With a payload capability of more than 37,000 pounds, which is only 5,000 less than a C-130, the C-160 has proved to be a durable workhorse. The Germans also won the 1987 Rodeo with one. Jim Dunn

Making the Rodeo even more competitive is the participation of teams from air forces of other nations. So far, teams from Europe, Asia, Australia, the Middle East, and South America have attended, and several of these teams have taken home the title of "World's Best Airlifters."

The first Volant Rodeo competition was held at Pope Air Force Base, North Carolina, in 1979. Pope was chosen because of its location next to the Army's Ft. Bragg, home of the famous 82nd Airborne Division. Here, there would be no trouble getting the large numbers of paratroopers needed for some of the Rodeo events.

Besides paratroopers, Ft. Bragg also provided wide open spaces for airdrop events and several unique dirt landing fields for the assault landing event. Named for World War II battlefields, such as Sicily and Luzon, these assault landing fields were used by C-130 Hercules and C-160 Transalls in the Rodeo's most exciting event. These bone jarring landings would often end with the aircraft completely disappearing in a thick red dust cloud.

Over the years, units flying the C-130, C-160 and C-141 Starlifter have been the mainstay of Rodeo competitions. However, the first couple of Rodeos also saw units equipped with C-7 Caribou and C-123 Providers, and in 1992, aerial refueling and navigation events were added for KC-10 Extenders and KC-135 Stratotankers. This was done because most tankers, including these two types of aircraft, had been transferred from Air Combat Command (ACC) to the control of Air Mobility Command (AMC), the successor to MAC.

In 1993, KC-10 and KC-135 teams competed in additional events making them eligible for the General William G. Moore Jr. Trophy, which is awarded to the overall Rodeo champion. The C-5 Galaxy also entered the competition in 1993, and the now renamed Airlift Rodeo features almost every type of mission in the airlift field.

Flying events that contribute points toward the Best Aircrew award vary greatly depending on the type of aircraft involved. For example, the C-130/C-160 aircrews are judged on airdrops and short field landings, while C-141 aircrews compete in airdrops and aerial refueling as receiver aircraft. Cargo loading also is an aircrew event for KC-10 and KC-135 teams.

Airdrops may be the most difficult flying events at the Rodeo. Crews are scored for timing and accuracy after flying a specific course with several checkpoints en route. Three flights are made during the Rodeo with a different load on each. Paratroopers are dropped from 800 feet, while heavy equipment and containers are dropped from 500 feet. It takes the combined skills of pilot, navigator, and loadmaster to achieve a high score in this event. Each of the airdrop flights ends with a short-field landing on a paved surface. Maximum points are scored by landing on a target 200 feet into the touchdown zone without bouncing.

Once the aircraft is on the ground, the aerial port crews go into action. If cargo must be lifted into a hostile area, time on the ground is the most dangerous period for an aircraft. This means loading and unloading the aircraft must be accomplished quickly with its engines still running.

Even Marine aviators know how to get down and dirty. On the dirt landing fields of Ft. Bragg, North Carolina, C-130s and C-160s took part in the Rodeo's short field landing competition. KC-130F (148899) is seen during the 1990 Rodeo, which was the last time the event was held on dirt landing fields. The Marines and other competitors will return to the dirt in 2000, when the Rodeo is once again held at Pope AFB. Jim Dunn

At the Rodeo, this type of operation is known as the Engines Running On/Offload (ERO) competition. This popular spectator event involves the team's aircraft taxiing into position, then being loaded with a truck and two trailers by a four-member team. The aircraft is then unloaded, and it departs the area. Speed is important, but major points are deducted for safety infractions.

Perhaps the area most overlooked in any operation is maintenance. These crews are responsible for having the aircraft ready to fly the mission and score points for the team. Aircraft preflight and postflight inspections, ground refueling, and daily observations are all judged. The Best of Maintenance award goes to a team in each of the aircraft types competing at the Rodeo.

All of this creates a spirited atmosphere of teamwork and camaraderie. A colorful tent city with unit and international flags flying is the social center of the Rodeo. Here, teams can relax and also carry on a brisk trade in unit patches and pins.

In the 15 Rodeo competitions held through 1996, active duty U.S. Air Force units have won eight times, while a USAF Reserve unit has two wins, and an Air National Guard unit has one victory. The winning teams flew the C-130 aircraft six times and C-141s three times. The big surprise is that KC-135 teams have won two of the three Rodeos in which they have competed.

Foreign teams also have made good use of the Rodeo to demonstrate their skills at airlift. Most of these teams used either C-130 or C-160 aircraft in the competition, though smaller transports, such as the Aeritalia G-222 and the CN-235, have been used in some events.

In 1982 and 1984, a team from Italy won the overall championship using a C-130; a West German team came home first with a C-160 in 1987; while a team from Australia won with a C-130 in 1989. Teams from New Zealand, Portugal, and Israel also have won the coveted title of Best C-130/C-160 Aircrew.

Ground and security personnel also play a big role in Rodeo competition. Many of the events they participate in simulate operations in a hostile environment. One event begins with establishing command and control of the airfield prior to the start of airlift operations. A Combat Control/Special Tactics Team makes a high altitude/low opening parachute jump into the area. They must establish a landing zone within 20 minutes, which includes setting up four different radios and taking wind measurements.

Other Rodeo events in this area include rifle and handgun marksmanship competitions, a biathlon, and obstacle courses. Teamwork plays a big part, as many of these events are not scored until the last member of the team crosses the finish line.

Like most things in the post-Cold War military, the Airlift Rodeo has undergone some major alterations in recent years. The first of these changes came just prior to the 1992 competition when control of Pope Air Force Base was transferred from AMC to Air Combat Command. Consequently, disruptions occurred during the competition that affected some of the flying events.

The Rodeo left Pope Air Force Base after the 1992 event, so assault landings are no longer part of the competition, nor are the accuracy landings for the C-141. These types of landings were taking a heavy toll on the aging airframes of the Starlifters. AMC made a quick decision to hold the 1993 Rodeo at its C-130 training ground at Little Rock Air Force Base, Arkansas. Later, McChord Air Force Base, Washington was designated as the Airlift Rodeo's new permanent home. At McChord, they would once again have plenty of paratroopers—this time from the 75th Ranger Regiment of the 1st Special Forces Group from Ft. Lewis, Washington.

After the 1994 event, AMC announced that the Rodeo would become a biennial competition held every even-numbered year. This reduced costs and also put the Rodeo on the same schedule as Gunsmoke and William Tell.

Just when it looked like all the changes were complete, the Air Force made a surprise announcement regarding Pope Air Force Base. In 1997, control of Pope was returned to AMC after nearly five years with ACC. It did not take long for AMC to return the Airlift Rodeo to Pope for 2000.

Other changes are likely to be seen in the types of competing aircraft. The C-17 will be present in larger numbers, and the venerable C-141 will pass into history. Even the C-130 Hercules will get a new look when the C-130J makes its debut.

As future Defense budgets tighten and fewer personnel are assigned more duties, it becomes even more important for policy makers to effectively gauge the morale of their forces. Some have viewed competitions like the Airlift Rodeo as an added burden on units and a drain on training funds.

For those who hold that opinion, visiting the event might change their minds. It would be impossible to miss the high spirits, camaraderie, and unit pride in evidence at the Rodeo. Competition does indeed bring out the best in a person and a team.

The General William G. Moore Jr. Trophy is proudly displayed in front of this hastily decorated C-141B, 66-0184, which was used by the 63rd MAW from Norton AFB, California, to win the 1990 Airlift Rodeo. It was only the second victory for a Starlifter unit in 11 competitions. Since then, only one other Starlifter unit has won the Airlift Rodeo, and the 63rd MAW and Norton AFB have both passed into history. Jim Dunn

continued from page 27

"B" Model Modifications and Operations

Having gained operational experience with the Starlifter, the Air Force determined that the aircraft had the power to carry a larger payload and the only thing restricting it was the aircraft's fuselage length. Funds were allocated to modify the entire C-141 fleet, 270 aircraft, with a fuselage extension of 23 feet, 4 inches and the addition of an in-flight refueling capability. All modified aircraft were redesignated as C-141Bs. C-141A serial number 66-186 was selected as the C-141B prototype. A 13-foot, 4-inch fuselage plug was added in front of the wing and a 10-foot plug was installed behind it, thereby increasing the cargo compartment's volume to 11,399 cubic feet—a boost of nearly 75 percent. The second C-141B to be modified, and the first to enter squadron service, was delivered to the 57th Military Air Transportation Squadron based at Altus Air Force Base, Oklahoma in January 1980.

C-141s from Travis, McChord, Norton, Charleston, and McGuire Air Force Bases all supported Operation Urgent Fury, the August 24, 1983, invasion of the island nation of Grenada. U.S. citizens attending medical school on the island were rescued, and the government was restored to a democracy during an eight-day assault in which 19 U.S. servicemen were killed and 116 wounded.

The action to oust Panamanian dictator General Manuel Noriega and restore democracy to the Latin American nation began on December 20, 1989, as Operation Just Cause. Starlifters flew paratroopers from stateside staging locations at Lawson and Hunter Army Air Fields in Georgia, Pope Air Force Base, North Carolina, and Charleston Air Force Base, South Carolina. Sixty-three C-141s, 21 C-130s and two C-5 Galaxies were used in the initial assault. More than 2,000 men of Fort Bragg, North Carolina's 82nd Airborne Division jumped

In the sensitive years following the end of the Cold War, several Starlifter units retained a few aircraft in the white-over-gray color scheme. These aircraft were used for diplomatic missions and flights into countries where this more civilian look was preferred. C-141B (67-0031) was on call with the 60th MAW at Travis AFB for these types of missions. *Jim Dunn*

One of these sensitive missions is seen coming to an end in the shadow of the Travis AFB control tower. Known in the Air Force as a Repatriation Flight, the remains of a U.S. serviceman is returned home from Vietnam. Chances are that this serviceman departed for Vietnam from the terminal at Travis AFB. *Carl E. Porter*

from C-141s to air assault their primary objective, Panama City's Omar Torrijos International Airport. Seven days after the assault began, 14 C-141s and eight C-5s began flying humanitarian aid to the people of Panama. In one week, they delivered three tons of medical supplies, two million field rations, 10,000 sheets and blankets, and several tons of dietary staples and baby food. Eight Starlifters and one C-130 later evacuated 257 injured U.S. military personnel from Panama's Howard Air Force Base to Kelly Air Force Base in Texas for further medical attention. Operation Just Cause proved to be the largest airdrop since World War II.

Volant Wind Sets the Stage to Battle Iraq

During the pre-dawn hours of August 2, 1990, 140,000 Iraqi troops equipped with tanks invaded the oil-rich Emirate of Kuwait. The temperature at 2 A.M. was over 100 degrees Fahrenheit as the

This C-141B is one of 13 that has been modified for a Special Operations Low-Level (SOLL) mission. These aircraft are fitted with forward-looking infrared (FLIR), infrared countermeasures system (IRCS), radar warning receiver (RWR), chaff/flare dispensers, secure communications equipment, head-up display (HUD), and special night vision cockpit light. All the aircraft are assigned to the 437th and 315th AW at Charleston AFB, South Carolina. *Jim Dunn*

The latest modification to the Starlifter fleet is represented by this glass cockpit on C-141C (65-9414). This aircraft is the first of 64 Starlifters that will be modified for Air Force Reserve and Air National Guard units. The new glass cockpit features an all-weather flight control system, GPS, a fuel-quantity indicating system, and the Airlift Defensive System. It was handed over to the 452nd Air Mobility Wing on October 31, 1997. *Jean Bizot*

Table II—C-141s Serial Numbers

Numbers Assigned	Total	Numbers Assigned	Total
61-2775/2779	(5)	66-0126/0209	(84)
63-8075/8090	(16)	66-7944/7959	(16)
64-0609/0653	(45)	67-0001/0031	(31)
65-0216/0281	(66)	67-0164/0166	(3)
65-9397/9414	(18)	Total	284*

Actual total of C-141s built is 285—one aircraft was built as a commercial prototype and eventually delivered to NASA.

invasion force headed across the desert sand toward the capital, Kuwait City. To deter Iraq from invading his nation, Saudi Arabia's King Fahd Ibn Abdul Aziz requested American assistance. On August 7, President George Bush ordered the implementation of Operation Desert Shield, tasked with deterring any further expansion plans Iraq might have, with restoring the legitimate Kuwaiti government by expelling Iraqi forces, and with protecting American citizens. That same day, the U.S. military's rapid deployment forces, consisting of the F-15 Eagle-equipped 1st Tactical Fighter Wing and the 2,300-man "ready brigade" of the 82nd Airborne Division, were dispatched to Saudi Arabia. Along with the United States, 26 other nations formed a coalition force, pooling economic and military resources to battle the Iraqis.

The Military Airlift Command's code name for the operation to supply Desert Shield's forces was dubbed Volant Wind. To move troops and supplies from America's East Coast to Saudi Arabia involved a 15-hour flight, usually with a stop at Rhein-Main Air Force Base in Germany, or at air bases in Spain. During the European stop, Starlifter crews would be relieved by fresh pilots and loadmasters for the nine-hour second leg across the Mediterranean to Saudi Arabia.

While diplomats attempted to persuade Iraq to withdraw its troops from Kuwait, the United Nations Security Council set a January 15, 1991, deadline for an Iraqi reply to its demands. On the day after the deadline passed, Operation Desert Shield changed to Desert Storm as coalition forces took the battle to Baghdad with air strikes. During the first 10 days of the offensive, coalition air forces flew more than 10,000 sorties, striking Iraqi military targets such as airfields, command and control centers, radar and missile launch sites, as well as tanks and troop emplacements.

Forty-five days later, on February 27, Kuwait was liberated in a lightning ground attack, but it was not until April 11, 1991, that Saddam Hussein agreed to the surrender terms of U.N. Security Council Resolution 678.

During Operations Desert Shield/Storm, 482,000 passengers were transported into or out of the theater of operations, 15 air-transportable hospitals with a 750-bed capacity made the long journey, and 513,000 tons of cargo was delivered. In just six weeks, this movement of materiel equaled the tonnage involved during the yearlong Berlin Airlift. While accomplishing this transportation of personnel and supplies, 80 percent of the Air Force's Starlifter fleet was deployed.

Twilight of the Starlifter

Aside from its military duties, C-141 Starlifters have been a lifeline to scientific stations on the Antarctic continent under Operation Deep Freeze. Starlifters also played a role in delivering famine relief supplies to Ethiopia, Sudan, Liberia, and Kurdish refugees in Iraq; in carrying humanitarian aid to Soviet Armenia after a devastating earthquake in 1987; in providing disaster relief to residents of Florida, Guam, and Hawaii struck by violent storms; in delivering medical supplies to Somalia; as well as in carrying food to the starving residents of Bosnia. Starlifters also support the United Nations peacekeeping efforts around the globe.

Years after the end of the Vietnam and Korean wars, Starlifters are still involved in those conflicts. C-141s have been tasked with the honor of bringing home America's war dead. America's goal is to account for each missing soldier. To that end, the nation employs teams of searchers to scour former battlefields. Also, when a former enemy nation discovers the remains of missing American servicepersons, honor guards are flown aboard C-141s to bring our soldiers home.

Lockheed had proposed a Service Life Extension Program (SLEP) for the C-141, but this has been deemed uneconomical and C-17s will replace the aging fleet of Starlifters. The type is expected to be retired from the Air Force's inventory in 2006.

3 Giant of the Airways
Lockheed's C-5 Galaxy

The evolution of military airlifters took another step forward in late 1961. The Military Air Transport Service (MATS) saw the success of Boeing's C-135 Stratolifter and knew that the future of airlift rested with its C-141 Starlifter, then under development.

Realizing that a jet-powered replacement for its turboprop-powered C-133 would be needed in the near future, MATS issued a quantitative operational requirement for a C-133 replacement. In October 1961, Lockheed engineers began to put ideas down on paper to formulate a concept of what this new giant cargo plane would look like. Pre-concept configuration studies examined design options for fuselage, wing, flap, engine nacelle and thrust reverser, landing gear, and cargo loading.] When the Specific Operational Requirement was released, it was clear a new airlifter was needed. The Air Force wanted its new cargo plane to have the capability of carrying 100,000 to 130,000 pounds for 4,000 miles at a cruising speed not less than 506 miles per hour at 30,000 feet. The plane had to be able to take off or land on an unimproved air strip. The cargo compartment was to be 100 to 110 feet-long, 16 to 17.5 feet wide, 13.5 feet tall, capable of straight-through loading, and the floor should be at truck-bed height, eliminating the need for special ground cargo handling equipment. The Air Force wanted the aircraft to be available by June 1970.

For the basic aircraft, Lockheed studied a four-engine T-tail design; another with the wing

June 30, 1998, marked the 30th anniversary of the first flight of the C-5A. Squadron service began in June 1970, when the 437th MAW at Charleston AFB, South Carolina, received the first Galaxy for operations. Of the 81 C-5As delivered, 76 remain in service, with two of those being converted to C-5Cs. High-time C-5A is 68-0214 with 19,133 hours, while low-time is C-5C, 68-0216, with 11,127 hours. *Jim Dunn*

The appearance of wing cracks early in testing led to a payload restriction of only 50,000 pounds. In 1973, the Yom Kippur War would give the Galaxy a chance to prove its capabilities. Without landing rights in Europe, our only way to supply Israel in time was with an unrestricted C-5 airlift. Operation Nickel Grass saw 10,800 tons of supplies delivered nonstop by C-5s, with the average flight carrying 74 tons. *Jim Dunn*

mounted low on the fuselage and four tail-mounted engines, similar in appearance to the British VC-10; a low-wing configuration with four underwing engines; a tailless Canard design with winglets; a Lambda Wing proposal; and a design featuring buried engines, much like the De Havilland Comet jet airliner. Lockheed settled on the conventional four-engine T-tail design, with clam-shell rear loading doors. However, to comply with the Air Force's straight-through loading requirement, three front entrance configurations were examined—one where the entire nose of the aircraft swung to the right; a second where the flight deck was above the cargo compartment and the lower nose swung to the right; and the design that was eventually selected—a raised cab

where the flight deck is above the cargo compartment and the nose swings upward.

In June 1964, having reviewed a number of pre-concept proposals, the Air Force Systems Command awarded contracts to Boeing, Douglas, and Lockheed to build a prototype for its CX-HLS (Cargo Experimental-Heavy Logistics System) aircraft. Contracts were also let to Pratt & Whitney and General Electric for CX-HLS powerplant designs. Lockheed submitted its "Model 500," featuring the T-tail with raised cab and upward-swinging visor nose. On October 1, 1965, after careful review, the Lockheed design was selected, and the company was contracted to build 81 heavy logistics aircraft under the designation C-5A Galaxy. General Electric won the engine-design competition with its TF-39-GE-1, the world's first 40,000 pound thrust high-bypass-ratio turbofan. The plane resembled its smaller cousin, the C-141 Starlifter, with its long fuselage, T-tail, and 25 degree swept wings. Despite its visual similarity, the C-5A dwarfed everything in the sky.

The Galaxy's interior contains three major compartments:

• The flight deck with pilot, co-pilot, and flight engineer stations, plus a relief crew area with six bunks and seven seats. There is also a courier compartment with eight seats, a galley, and a lavatory.

• Behind the wing on the upper deck is the troop compartment with seating for 73 troops and two jumpmasters, a galley, and lavatories.

• The cargo compartment is capable of handling vehicles, helicopters, and palletized cargo. The level floor area is 121 feet, 1 inch long by 19 feet wide and 13 feet, six inches tall. Two ramps add an additional 23 feet, 6 inches of cargo space. The total volume of cargo space is 34,795 cubic feet—five times greater than the C-141.

Both the forward and rear cargo doors incorporate self-contained ramp systems, eliminating the need for ground support equipment. The cavernous cargo bay can accommodate 348 grand pianos, or six Greyhound passenger buses, or eight bowling alley lanes, or six AH-64 Apache

The C-5 Galaxy's lower cargo area is more than 40 yards long and 6 yards wide. It can be configured to carry troops, mechanized equipment, a helicopter, an M1 Abrams main battle tank, or a mix of all of these. That type of versatility is unmatched by any other plane operating with any other air force on Earth. *Jim Dunn*

To power an aircraft the size of the Galaxy, new developments in engine technology were required. In the first use of a high-bypass-ratio turbofan engine, General Electric YTF39-GE-1s were fitted for initial test flights. These 41,000-pound military thrust engines were successful, and the TF39-GE-1 was adopted for the C-5A. The uprated TF39-GE-1C, producing 43,000 pounds of thrust, was later produced for the C-5B. *Jim Dunn*

Each of the C-5's engine nacelles has a diameter of more than 8 feet 6 inches, measures 27 feet long, and weighs 7,900 pounds. The Galaxy has an empty operating weight of 374,000 pounds. More often than not, it is the weight of the C-5 and not its size that restricts operations. Even at many USAF bases, the C-5 is often limited to a single ramp area. *Jim Dunn*

helicopters, or six M-2/M-3 Bradley infantry vehicles, or one of the Army's 74-ton mobile bridging systems. Since every airlift milestone and airlift plane must be compared to its brethren of the Berlin Airlift, only 17 C-5s would have been required to fly the entire airlift—an operation that required 308 aircraft for nearly one year.

Externally, the C-5 has a number of unique features. Its landing gear has 24 main wheels in four six-wheel bogeys and a steerable, four-wheel nose gear. The main landing gear struts can be raised or lowered individually for wheel and brake changes, and a pneumatic system provides air which allows the tires to be serviced without

Provided there is a parking area that can accommodate its weight, chances are the C-5 can deal with the local ground support equipment. Front and rear loading and unloading of cargo is available using the full-width ramps at both ends. The C-5 also can use its ability to kneel to meet the height of various trucks or K-loaders. *Jim Dunn*

ground equipment. Each gear leg has a hydraulically operated kneeling device to lower the fuselage, allowing simultaneous cargo loading from both the front and rear entrances. The raised-cab flight deck and upward swinging nose visor make the Galaxy a unique sight while unloading cargo. Its tall tail reaches as high as a six-story building, and behind the cockpit, on top of the fuselage, is the C-5's aerial refueling receptacle.

Entering the Inventory

The first C-5A, serial number 68-8303, rolled out of Lockheed's Marietta, Georgia, factory on March 2, 1968. Leo J. Sullivan, pilot, and Walter E. Hensleigh, co-pilot, were at the controls when 68-8303 made its first flight, which lasted 94 minutes, on June 30, 1968. The Air Force Military Airlift Command's 443rd Military Airlift Wing received its first aircraft on December 17, 1969, at Altus Air Force Base, Oklahoma, for crew training. The 443rd provided transition training on the C-5A, introducing new crews to the giant airlifter.

Once the C-5A became operational, it flew its first mission to Vietnam on July 9, 1970. The behemoth was originally limited to landing at Cam Ranh Bay but, after runway and aerial port expansion programs, was eventually able to use Tan Son Nhut and others. The C-5's cargo-carrying capability was so large that once its payload was offloaded, it had to be reloaded on pallets and then trans-

Without the benefit of a C-5 airlift, some aircraft in the Air Force Museum system would never make it to display status. Aircrews also benefit from the training they receive when called on to transport these unusual loads. This HU-16 Albatross was airlifted from Luke AFB, Arizona, to the museum at McClellan AFB, California, by a crew from the 433rd Airlift Wing, Kelly AFB, Texas. *Jim Dunn*

This type of landing is not recommended for any aircraft, let alone a C-5. Making a rather inauspicious entrance at the 1994 Rodeo at McChord AFB, this crew from Dover AFB had its C-5 standing up on its four nosegear tires. The Galaxy has a total of 28 wheels to support its weight, with four main bogies of six wheels each plus the four-wheel nosegear. *Jim Dunn*

shipped by C-130s to in-country destinations. When Da Nang was under siege in 1972, ten C-5 sorties brought 1,650,000 pounds of tanks, helicopters, and other supplies into Vietnam. These cargoes were unloaded during ERO (Engine Running-Offload) conditions. Each C-5 was emptied in just 32 minutes to limit its exposure to enemy fire.

On May 18, 1973, three months before the end of America's offensive operations in Viet-nam, the last of 81 C-5As was delivered to the Air Force. In August, C-5s participated in Operation Enhance Plus to supply the South Vietnamese Air Force with the final deliveries of aircraft and helicopters in anticipation of the American military withdrawal from the country.

When Israel was attacked on October 6, 1973, C-5s supported America's ally in its effort to win the Yom Kippur War. During Operation Nickel Grass,

Table I—C-5B Galaxy Specifications

Length:	247 feet, 10 inches
Wing Span:	222 feet, 8.5 inches
Height:	65 feet, 1.5 inches
Empty Weight:	374,000 pounds
Maximum Takeoff Weight:	837,000 pounds
Operating Weight:	374,000 pounds
Maximum Payload:	261,000 pounds
Maximum Cruising Speed:	.77 Mach
Maximum Speed:	.825 Mach
Unrefueled Range with Max. Payload:	3,434 miles
Powerplants:	Four General Electric TF-39-GE-1C turbofan engines rated at 43,000 pounds thrust each
Total Fuel Capacity:	51,154 gallons
Crew:	Seven (pilot, co-pilot, two flight engineers, and three loadmasters)

C-5s delivered 10,800 tons of tanks, artillery, ammunition, and other supplies in 145 sorties.

The tremendous carrying capability of the Galaxy made it an excellent choice for Operation Babylift, the effort to evacuate more than 2,000 Vietnamese American orphans to the United States. Sadly, on April 4, 1975, C-5A 68-0218 crashed near Saigon shortly after takeoff from Tan Son Nhut. A rear door blew out, damaging hydraulic and control lines. While attempting to return to the air base nearly out of control, the aircraft crashed killing 155, mostly children, of the 314 souls on board. More would have perished had it not been for pilot Dennis Traylor's exceptional skill.

C-5 Modifications

To extend the life of the C-5 and cure a wing crack problem that was limiting the amount of cargo carried, a wing strengthening modification was planned. The contract to design an upgrade was signed in December 1975 between the Air Force and Lockheed. In January 1978, the Air Force approved the construction of two new wing sets, one that would be statically tested to its destruction, and the other flown in C-5A 68-0214. The wing modification replaced the center wing torsion box and two inner wing and two outer wing box sections. However, it retained the leading and trailing edge elements including the flaps and ailerons. A new aluminum alloy, 7175-T73511, unavailable in the 1960s, gives the modified C-5A wing its strength. The production-line retrofit of new wings for all C-5As began in July

It takes as much skill and teamwork to taxi a C-5 as it does to fly one. Sitting more than 25 feet off the ground, the two pilots are assisted by at least two observers standing behind them on the flight deck. Those on the ground directing the aircraft must pay special attention to remain in sight of the pilots and the more than 222-foot wingspan of the C-5. *Jim Dunn*

The airdrop capabilities of the C-5 were best demonstrated on an overcast June 7, 1989, at Ft. Bragg, North Carolina. A new world's record was set when C-5B (86-0017) airdropped a payload of 190,493 pounds, consisting of 73 paratroopers and four M551 Sheridan tanks, which required eight G-11 parachutes each for descent. *Jim Dunn*

With everything down and "hanging," this C-5 is seen on final approach to McClellan AFB, California. Gear down, leading edge slats extended, and modified Fowler trailing edge flaps deployed, the C-5 was designed to meet the requirements of landing with a 125,000-pound payload on a 4,000-foot, semi-prepared surface. Only during testing at Edwards AFB in California has a C-5 made a landing on a dirt surface. *Jim Dunn*

Travis-based C-5A (69-0027) catches the morning sun off the Oregon coast during a training mission to requalify crews in air refueling. This view shows the detail in the camouflage paint scheme that C-5s wore throughout the 1980s and early 1990s. While best for operations in Europe and Asia, this scheme had major drawbacks in other locations. Now AMC has adopted an overall gray scheme for its C-5 and C-141 fleet. *Rene J. Francillon*

1981 and included the replacement of the aircraft's monochrome weather radar with upgraded, full-color displays. The final rewinged C-5A was delivered to the Air Force on July 7, 1986.

Two C-5As (68-0213 and 68-0216) were converted to a Space Container Transport System (SCTS) configuration with the removal of the upper deck troop seating area behind the wing, the relocation of the flap/slat asymmetry control box to the courier compartment forward of the wing, and the expansion of the planes' rear cargo doors. This allows outsize loads to be delivered to Cape Canaveral, Florida, in support of the Space Shuttle program, and to Vandenberg Air Force Base, California, for missile testing. Both Galaxies are stationed at Travis Air Force Base, California.

In the mid-1990s, C-5s underwent another modification project known as Pacer Snow—a defensive countermeasures retrofit giving a number of C-5s Tracor-built AN/ALE-40 flare dispensers as well as a Honeywell AN/AAR-47 missile warning system.

New C-5s to Increase Airlift Capacity

Simultaneous to the wing upgrade, the Air Force reviewed the potential for acquiring additional C-5s. Lockheed still held the original tooling in storage; thus it was only a matter of money. But none was available and the tooling remained in storage, collecting dust. In 1981, the Air Force undertook a Congressionally-mandated review of military airlift needs, which recommended the purchase of additional aircraft. Seeing an opening, Lockheed took it upon itself to submit a proposal to the Air Force for the purchase of 50 new C-5s for a fixed price. By December 1982, Lockheed had been awarded a contract for the production of 50 aircraft, designated C-5B. Production began in April 1984. These aircraft would incorporate the

Table II—
C-5 Galaxy Serial Numbers

C-5A		C-5B	
66-8303/8307	(5)	82-1285	(1)
67-167/174	(8)	84-0059/0062	(4)
68-211/228	(18)	85-0001/0010	(10)
69-001/027	(27)	86-0011/0026	(16)
		87-0027/0045	(19)

"A" model's strengthened wing, use more powerful 43,000 pound static thrust General Electric TF39-GE-IC engines, and incorporate the latest technology avionics including an improved Automatic Flight Control System (AFCS) and an updated Malfunction Detection and Analysis

An additional production run of the Galaxy in the late 1980s produced 50 C-5Bs for the USAF. Improvements included the already designed strengthened wing box, slightly more powerful engines, and stronger aluminum alloys and fasteners. C-5B (87-0040) returns to its parking space at Travis AFB after a mission on April 1, 1998, that added a few more hours to the nearly 9,000 already in its logbook. *Jim Dunn*

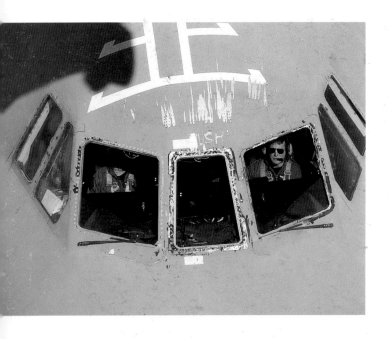

Aerial refueling of the Galaxy presents challenges for both crews. With the KC-135, it is the massive bow wave created by the C-5 that is the problem, while C-5 crews have difficulty with the tail-mounted engine of the KC-10. The boomers on *Quest 52*, a KC-10 of the 70th ARS at Travis AFB, want everyone to know that they were not responsible for the battered condition of this C-5. *Jim Dunn*

Recording system (MADAR II). The first C-5B, 83-1285, was rolled out at Marietta on July 12, 1985, and flew for the first time on September 10, 1985. C-5B 83-1285 was delivered to the 443rd Military Airlift Wing at Altus Air Force Base, Oklahoma on January 8, 1986, and the 50th and final C-5B was accepted by the 436th Military Airlift Wing, Dover Air Force Base, Delaware, on April 17, 1989.

Galaxies have been active in every military and civilian action in recent history. Two days after an earthquake struck Mexico City in 1985, C-5s and C-141s from Travis Air Force Base started an airlift totaling 190 tons of supplies to the area. In December 1988, four C-5s participated in the delivery of more than 885,000 pounds of supplies to Armenia after that nation was struck by an extremely strong earthquake. During the March 1989 ecological disaster known as the *Exxon Valdez* oil spill, C-5s delivered almost two million pounds of equipment to Elmendorf Air Force Base, Alaska, to aid in the clean-up efforts. Supplies were flown to areas in the Caribbean hit by Hurricane Hugo in September 1989, and by South Florida's Hurricane Andrew in August 1992.

A little known variant of the Galaxy is the C-5C. Two C-5As (68-0213 and 68-0216) were converted by removing the 73-seat upper passenger deck. This increased the cargo area aft of the wing, and along with modifications to the rear loading doors, it allowed these aircraft to carry special loads designed for the Space Shuttle. Both aircraft are assigned to the 60th Air Mobility Wing at Travis AFB. *Jim Dunn*

Except for the "horn button' identifying this as a C-5C (68-0213), this cockpit is the same as that of any C-5A. A program is now underway to upgrade the C-5A fleet with the avionics subsystems developed for the C-5B, which includes a modernized flight management system, GPS receivers, triple Internal Navigation System (INS), and color weather radar. *Jim Dunn*

Operation Desert Shield/Storm saw 95 percent of the Air Force's C-5s devoted to supplying the Kuwaiti theater of operations. C-5s flew 42 percent of the cargo and 18.6 percent of the passenger missions to supply the operation.

During the famine relief efforts in Somalia within the first months of 1993, C-5s delivered soldiers and materiel to the capital city of Mogadishu. Altogether, Air Force airlifters, including C-5s, would fly 855 sorties in support of Operation Restore Hope, the largest humanitarian airlift ever undertaken.

Air Mobility Command will rely upon its fleet of C-5 Galaxies for many years to come, providing worldwide delivery of both military and humanitarian cargo. Eventually, all C-5As will have the C-5B's cockpit avionics package installed, and all C-5s are in the process of having their flight management systems modernized and Global Positioning System (GPS) receivers installed. The Air Force has begun operations with the Boeing C-17 Globemaster III which will replace the C-141 Starlifter and supplement the C-5 fleet well into the next century.

4 KC-10A Extender
Airlifter and Aerial Refueler

n the mid-1970s, the Air Force developed a specification for an Advanced Tanker Cargo Aircraft (ATCA). An aircraft was needed to deliver fuel in-flight in order to increase the range of other aerial combatants, and provide the flexibility to deliver troops and/or cargo to airfields with restricted lengths.

Boeing entered the competition with a modified four-engine 747 fitted with an aerial refueling boom, and McDonnell Douglas offered a militarized version of its DC-10-30CF (Convertible Freighter). On December 19, 1977, the Air Force selected McDonnell Douglas' entry for its ability to lift heavier loads and operate from shorter fields than the larger 747.

The DC-10-30 and -30CF is the intercontinental range version of the DC-10. Extending the airliner's range was accomplished by increasing the fuel load from 21,762 gallons to 37,747 gallons in the extended range -30 models. On the fuselage centerline under the wing, a third main landing-gear leg with two wheels was added to distribute the -30's increased weight. This main gear could be selectively deployed depending upon the aircraft's loaded weight. The -30CF also featured a 140-inch by 102-inch side cargo door on the left front fuselage allowing container stowage on the main cabin floor. Commercial operators of the -30CF included Continental Airlines, Sabena Airlines, World Airways, Federal Express, Overseas National Airways, Transamerica Airlines, and Martinair-Holland.

The introduction of the KC-10 Extender represented a major increase in the capabilities of the tanker/transport fleet. In its primary tanker role, the addition of in-flight refueling gives the KC-10 a huge advantage over the total fuel capacity of 31,275 gallons for the KC-135. Add the ability to carry twice the payload of the KC-135A, and the Extender becomes an important asset in the transport role. *Rene J. Francillon*

The commercial DC-10-30CF became the military KC-10A Extender by incorporating the following modifications:

- The main cabin floor was strengthened to handle 169,409 pounds of cargo.
- The lower front and rear luggage bays were filled with bladder-type tanks to provide fuel for other planes.
- A boom operator's position and refueling boom was incorporated in a ventral position on the rear fuselage centerline.
- A hose-and-drogue refueling nozzle system was fitted on the starboard lower rear fuselage.
- An aerial refueling receptacle was installed in a dorsal position behind the cockpit.

The inclusion of both boom-type refueling systems (used exclusively by Air Force aircraft) and the hose-and-drogue refueling nozzle (used by the Navy and foreign air arms) made the Extender extremely versatile in the types of aircraft it could service.

The total fuel capacity of the KC-10A is 54,455 gallons, of which 30,000 gallons can be transferred to receiver aircraft. This allows the tanker to fly approximately 2,200 miles, orbit and dispense 30,000 gallons of fuel, and return to base with an adequate safety margin. The boom operator manipulates a McDonnell Douglas' fly-by-wire Advanced Aerial Refueling Boom (AARB) that can off-load 1,500 gallons per minute.

In addition to the factory-installed hose-and-drogue refueling point, 40 Extenders have been retrofitted with removable hose-and-drogue nozzles in under-wing pods, enabling the KC-10A to refuel three aircraft simultaneously. These nozzles can pour 600 gallons per minute into receiver aircraft.

The first KC-10A, serial number 79-0433, flew from the company's Long Beach, California,

The KC-10 Extender owes much of its heritage to the commercial DC-10, especially the DC-10-30CF. Powered by three General Electric CF6-50C2 engines rated at 52,500 pounds thrust each, the KC-10 also features a reinforced cargo deck and upward hinged cargo door. In all, 88 percent of its systems are in common with the DC-10. *Jim Dunn*

While its principal mission is as a tanker, the KC-10 has proved to be a very versatile transport. With a usable cargo space over 12,000 cubic feet, it can carry 169,409 pounds a distance of 4,370 miles unrefueled. The 8 foot 6 inch by 11 foot 8 inch cargo door allows a vehicle like this military Humvee to be loaded during an Airlift Rodeo competition. *Jim Dunn*

Table I—KC-10A Extender Specifications

Length:	181 feet, 7 inches
Wing Span:	165 feet, 4.25 inches
Height:	58 feet, 1 inch
Empty Weight:	240,065 pounds
Maximum Weight:	590,000 pounds
Maximum Fuel Load:	356,000 pounds
Maximum Payload:	169,409 pounds— up to 75 persons, maximum of 27 pallets
Cruising Speed at 30,000 Feet:	564 miles per hour
Maximum Speed at 25,000 Feet:	610 miles per hour
Unrefueled Range with Max. Payload:	4,370 miles
Powerplants:	Three General Electric CF6-50C2 turbofans rated at 51,800 pounds thrust each
Crew:	Four (pilot, co-pilot, flight engineer, boom operator)
Cargo Capacity:	Seventy-five passengers on palletized seats plus 146,000 pounds of cargo on 17 pallets, or 27 pallets

factory on July 12, 1980. One year later, Extenders became operational with Barksdale Air Force Base, Louisiana's 32nd Air Refueling Squadron of the Strategic Air Command's 2nd Bombardment Wing, during October 1981. KC-10A operational readiness added another tool to the Strategic and Tactical Air Command's arsenal, enhancing its ability to show force at any point on the globe.

The KC-10A's baptism in combat came in the days leading up to and including April 15, 1986. On that day, U.S. Navy and Air Force aircraft struck alleged terrorist targets in Libya during Operation El Dorado Canyon. In response to numerous Libyan-sponsored acts of terrorism against American citizens and the bombing of Berlin's La Belle discotheque on April 5, 1986, the United States retaliated against Libyan military targets and those of suspected terrorists. Nineteen KC-10As from the 2nd Bombardment Wing, Barksdale Air Force Base, Louisiana, from

McDonnell Douglas designers first added the twin-wheel centerline undercarriage to the DC-10-30 model. This addition became a big selling point for the KC-10 as it greatly increased the fuel capacity and range of the aircraft without any reduction in size. The feature also helped the KC-10 obtain a maximum gross takeoff weight of 590,000 pounds. *Jim Dunn*

The original airline-style livery of the KC-10 is long gone. Also gone is much of the nose art that KC-10s carried while assigned to Strategic Air Command units. The tradition of painting nose art on an aircraft has never been a strong one in transport units, and with all KC-10s now in Air Mobility Command, there are far fewer still wearing nose art. *Jim Dunn*

the 68th Air Refueling Group from Seymour-Johnson Air Force Base, North Carolina; and from the 22nd Air Refueling Wing at March Air Force Base, California, began deploying aircraft to England's RAF Mildenhall and RAF Fairford on April 11 in preparation for the attack. An additional 34 KC-135s staged through Mildenhall and Fairford in support of Operation El Dorado Canyon.

Because France and Spain denied overflight permission, striking Air Force F-111F bombers from RAF Lakenheath and defense suppression EF-111A Ravens from RAF Upper Heyford had to fly around those nations, making a 5,500-mile round-trip mission. To maintain an element of surprise, all rendezvous and refuelings on the way to the target were done under complete radio silence. Due to the F-111's weapons load, four hook-ups were made with the tanker

Above a solid cloud deck at 20,960 feet over the Pacific, Maj. Dan McLucas and Maj. Isabel Kalocsay head their Extender to rendezvous with a C-5 to conduct a refueling training mission. The cockpit of the KC-10 features a triple INS with a Rockwell Collins FMS-800 flight management system that integrates INS and the GPS. *Jim Dunn*

KC-10A (87-0124) was delivered in November 1988, the last of 60 Extenders built. It was first used to test the British-built Mk32B hose drum pod that was fitted under each wing to make the KC-10 a three-point tanker. Now flying with the 305th Air Mobility Wing at McGuire AFB, it is the low-time KC-10 with 6,621 hours. High-time KC-10 is 79-1712 with 13,333 hours. *Jim Dunn*

With more than 650,000 hours in its logbooks, the KC-10 fleet has established one of the best safety records in USAF history. To date, only one aircraft has been written off in an accident. On Sept. 17, 1987 (KC-10A, 82-0190) was destroyed during a refueling on the ramp at Barksdale AFB. There were no fatalities, and the cause of the accident was improper procedures by ground personnel. *Jim Dunn*

force en route to the target, and two on the way back. The raid on Libya was extremely successful, destroying six Il-76 transports, one Boeing 727, two Fokker F.27s, four MiG-23 fighters, two Mi-8 helicopters, as well as the Al Jamahiriyah Barracks, and numerous other targets. Unfortunately, one F-111F was lost during the raid.

During Operation Just Cause, the 1986 military assault to restore democratic rule to Panama, KC-10s and KC-135s off-loaded 12 million-plus pounds of fuel to more than 100 aircraft during 256 sorties.

As part of the Air Force's Global Reach/ Global Power concept, KC-10s form one part of the Air Force Air Mobility Command's capability to deploy men and materiel around the globe and support them for any length of time. During

To support Operations Desert Shield and Desert Storm, 46 of the 59 KC-10s in service were deployed overseas. In Europe, they were based at Milan-Malpensa Airport, Italy, and Zaragoza Air Base, Spain. Those flying directly in support of combat missions operated out of Jeddah/King Abdul Aziz International Airport, Saudi Arabia. *Rene J. Francillon*

In recent years, downsizing and realignment have greatly changed the makeup of the USAF. Photographed at McChord AFB in June 1994, these KC-10s from Seymour Johnson AFB, North Carolina, and March AFB, California, are now assigned elsewhere. Today, all Extenders are located at either McGuire AFB, New Jersey, or Travis AFB, California. *Jim Dunn*

Another base that is no longer home to a KC-10 unit is Barksdale AFB, Louisiana. In October 1981, the 32nd Air Refueling Squadron at Barksdale became the first unit to operate the KC-10. The 32nd ARS was then part of the Strategic Air Command, as were the next three squadrons to receive Extenders. Now based at McGuire AFB, the 32nd ARS flies the KC-10 for Air Mobility Command. *Jim Dunn*

the decade of the 1990s, KC-10s have been extensively used to support America's troops in the Persian Gulf region. In Operation Desert Shield/Storm, 46 Extenders were deployed to the Persian Gulf region to support Coalition Forces. This combat situation demonstrated the KC-10A's flexibility to use both its flying boom and hose-and-drogue refueling points to service numerous types of aircraft from many nations. Air Force and Navy aircraft no longer needed a dedicated tanker to support the planes of each service.

In September 1996, KC-10s based at McGuire Air Force Base, New Jersey, supported F-117A Stealth fighters and B-52s that were redeployed to the Persian Gulf region to deter hostile Iraqi actions. When some of the troops came home in June 1998, KC-10s were there again as airborne filling stations, extending the range of troop transports flying from the Gulf to the United States. In November 1998, KC-10s once again flew men and supplies to the Persian Gulf region in a force build-up. This effort was another attempt to convince Iraqi leader Saddam Hussein to allow United Nations weapons inspectors to continue their efforts to monitor the country's capability to produce weapons of mass destruction.

Table II— KC-10A Serial Numbers

79-0433/-0434	(2)
79-1710-1713	(4)
79-1946/-1951	(6)
82-0190/-0193	(4)
83-0075/-0082	(8)
84-0185/-0192	(8)
85-0027/-0034	(8)
86-0027/-0038	(12)
87-0117/-0124	(8)

Looking over the shoulder of Capt. Mike Solomon as he lines up KC-10 84-0191 with Runway 21R at Travis AFB. Like many other Air Force Reserve pilots, Capt. Solomon also flies with an airline, a practice which allows the Air Force to maintain a high level of experience in its cockpits. *Jim Dunn*

About to take on fuel from a KC-135E, this KC-10 demonstrates its most important feature. With in-flight refueling and nearly twice the fuel capacity of the KC-135, the Extender lives up to its name by providing mission planners with many additional options. A single KC-10 receiving en route refueling can support up to eight fighters on a nonstop deployment. *Rene J. Francillon*

Ten years after the delivery of the final KC-10, it is clear that the order for only 60 aircraft was far too small. Even in a downsized military, the importance of a large tanker/transport cannot be understated. With the end of production for the MD-11 in sight, can the USAF live with a twin-engine tanker? If they don't act soon, this might be the only choice they have. *Rene J. Francillon*

KC-10s also helped two B-1B Lancers from the 7th Bomb Wing based at Dyess Air Force Base, Texas, set a record. The Lancers flew around-the-world in 36 hours, 13 minutes with the aid of aerial refueling—setting the record for fastest non-stop circumnavigation of the globe. During tests of the new Boeing C-17 Globemaster III, KC-10s from Travis Air Force Base, California, were used to demonstrate the new strategic airlifter's in-flight refueling capability.

Now that Boeing has acquired McDonnell Douglas, and the DC-10 and KC-10 production lines have been closed for years, other nations interested in an Extender type aircraft have begun to acquire commercial DC-10s for conversion to military transport configuration. The Netherlands acquired two ex-Martinair DC-10-30CFs that were modified by McDonnell Douglas with an in-flight refueling receptacle, wing-mounted hose-and-drogue reels capable of dispensing 400 gallons per minute, and a flying boom that off-loads 800 gallons per minute. These converted airliners have been designated KDC-10s. The main deck can accommodate 26 pallets or 300 passengers or a combination of the two. With more than 375 DC-10s and 59 KC-10s flying today, parts support will not be a factor for any nation wishing to acquire its own fleet of modern tankers at used aircraft prices.

Like the Extender, the aircraft chosen to replace the KC-135 will be both a tanker and a transport. AMC would like to have the KC-X enter service in 2013; however, the possibility of large scale corrosion within the KC-135 fleet may rush that date, making it far less likely the aircraft would be a new design. *Jim Dunn*

KC-10s continue to support U.S. military commitments and humanitarian efforts throughout the world. Extenders are flying to, or refueling aircraft en route to, countries such as Rwanda, Yugoslavia, Bosnia, and Kuwait. Extender crews may not get the same press as those flying Stealth fighters, but their mission is just as vital. Armies and aircraft move on fuel.

5

C-17 Globemaster III
High-Tech Cargo Carrier

Airlift operations during the Vietnam War demonstrated the Air Force's need for a large cargo-carrying aircraft capable of delivering its load directly to frontline forces. C-5s and C-141s brought supplies from the states to large, secure, well-prepared bases far behind the battle front, before off-loading and departing the area. Ground crews were then faced with the task of reconfiguring the cargo to fit aboard smaller C-130s for intra-theater delivery. This process delayed the arrival of men and materiel, and required large support forces at rear-echelon bases.

The ideal aircraft would be the size of a C-141, would be able to deliver loads comparable to a C-5, would not require large amounts of ground support equipment to load and unload supplies, and would be capable of air dropping supplies and deploying paratroops at the far limit of its endurance. A militarized airliner would not suffice, since its cargo deck is approximately 16 to 20 feet in the air, requiring special ground handling equipment. Thus, it would not be able to operate at a forward area with unprepared air strips. The ideal airlifter would be capable of roll-on, roll-off loading of tanks, vehicles, and other mobile cargo such as attack helicopters.

From this need, the Air Force began work on its Advanced Medium Short Takeoff/Landing Transport (AMST) in the early 1970s. Boeing and McDonnell Douglas each provided demonstrator aircraft, the YC-14 and YC-15 respectively. Although they never reached the production stage, they served as proof-of-concept aircraft showing that "powered lift devices" could dramatically

Globemaster IIIs are living up to their name as they are now being flown worldwide by crews from the 437th and 315th Airlift Wings based at Charleston AFB, South Carolina. The 437th AW is the active duty unit, while the 315th AW is part of Air Force Reserve Command (AFRC). AFRC became the ninth major command in the Air Force on February 17, 1997. *Greg L. Davis*

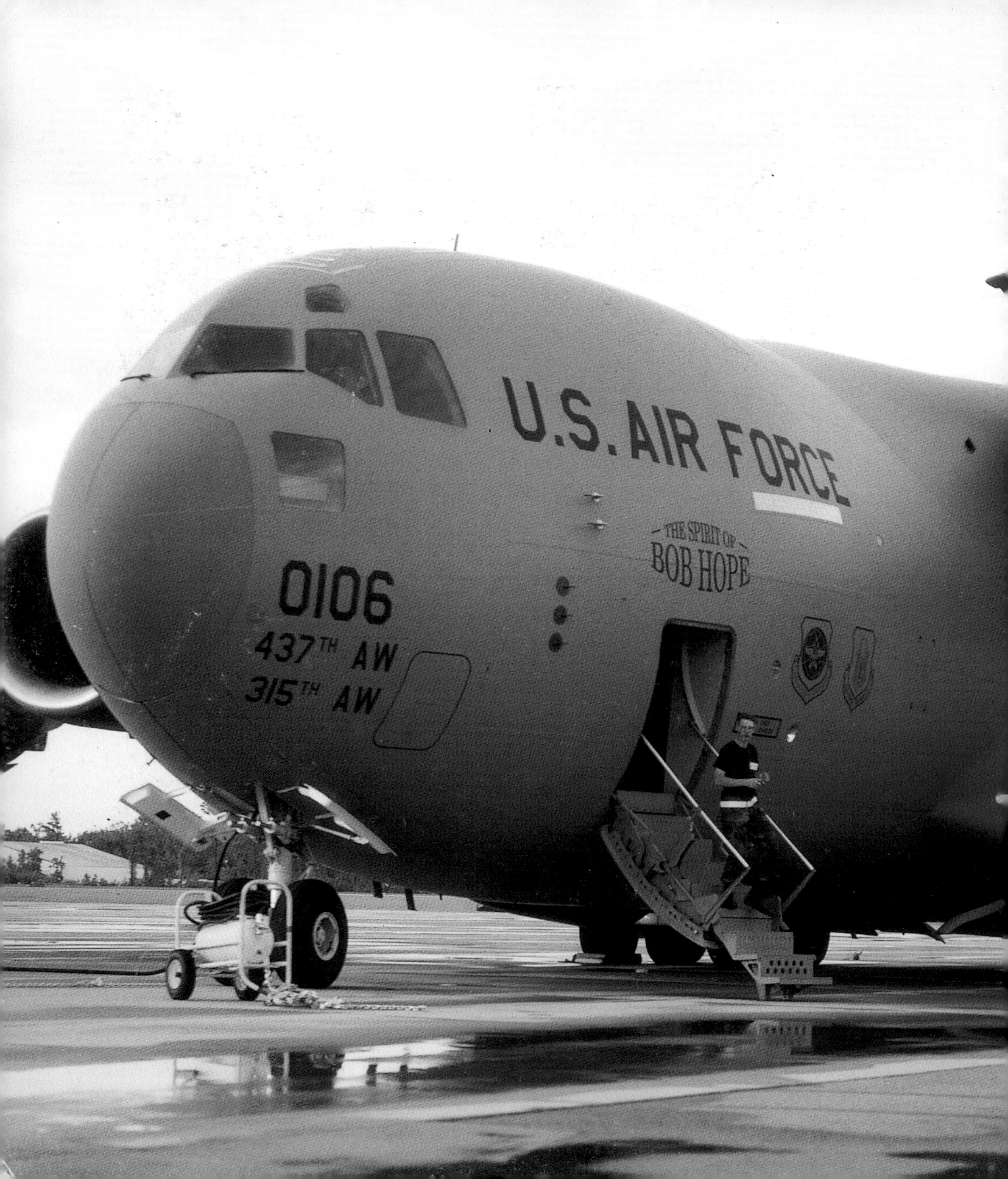
U.S. AIR FORCE
THE SPIRIT OF
BOB HOPE
0106
437TH AW
315TH AW

The state-of-the-art cockpit on the C-17 features a fly-by-wire control system that uses stick grips in place of the traditional control yoke. Each pilot has an all-functional heads-up display (HUD), and there are four cathode-ray tube (CRT) displays with conventional instruments as backup. One addition for aircraft flying into a combat zone, such as Bosnia, is that bullet-proof Kevlar panels have been laid down on the floor of the cockpit to protect the flight crew from small arms and light anti-aircraft fire when approaching or departing airports in hostile areas. *Jim Dunn*

reduce a fully loaded airlifter's takeoff run and landing roll. These reduced operating parameters opened up numerous austere landing fields to large cargo aircraft.

Following on the heels of the AMST program, the Air Force issued a request for proposals for its

Designed by McDonnell Douglas and now built under the Boeing name, the C-17 Globemaster III is set to play a major role in American military mobility for decades to come. At present, the C-17 fleet has surpassed 90,000 flight hours, and aircraft, such as 95-0106, *Spirit of Bob Hope,* are demonstrating the capabilities of the Globemaster III in a variety of airlift missions. *Greg L. Davis*

C-X airlifter program in October 1980. On August 28, 1981, McDonnell Douglas was selected to build the C-17 Globemaster III for the Air Force. In February 1985, full-scale development was authorized and a fixed-price incentive contract for $3.387 billion was issued at the end of the year. McDonnell Douglas was granted another $725 million for tooling in 1987.

Upon first glance, the C-17 resembles a C-141 in size, but advances in technology since the later plane's introduction to service put the C-17 in a class by itself. Like all primary airlifters, the aircraft has a T-tail above a rear loading ramp, a supercritical high-lift wing, full-span leading edge

Experience has shown that many overseas airlift operations must be conducted on small airfields with limited facilities. This is where the tight turning radius and unique thrust reversers on the C-17 come into play. The directed-flow thrust reversers direct engine thrust forward and up so that the C-17 can back up without disrupting operations on the airfield. *Jim Dunn*

slats, in-flight refueling capability, and externally blown flaps. The C-17's rear loading ramp is full-width and can accommodate simultaneous, double row loading. The aft door is one unit that opens internally allowing for outsize cargo to be loaded or for use of the low-altitude parachute extraction system. Side doors feature a paratrooper platform and wind deflectors built into the fuselage.

The wing's area is 3,800 square feet and has a 25-degree sweep angle. The winglets have a span of 9.21 feet with a 30-degree sweep angle and a vertical angle of 15 degrees.

Mounted under the wing are four 40,440-pound-thrust Pratt & Whitney F117-PW-100 turbofans that power the C-17. These engines pro-

Passenger seating differs somewhat from other military transport aircraft. The C-17 has 54 individual, permanently installed seats along the sidewalls and carries on board eight sets of six back-to-back seats. Another option is for 100 airline-type seats that can be loaded ten per pallet. Total capacity for an aeromedical evacuation is 48 litters plus 102 ambulatory. Here, 102 fully-equipped U.S. Marines demonstrate the loading for a paradrop at the Yuma proving grounds, Marine Corps Air Station, Yuma, Arizona. *Boeing*

vide so much thrust that with reversers deployed, they can back the plane up a two percent grade. The F117 engine has been proven during years of service on commercial airliners. The PW2040, its civilian designation, powers such jetliners as the Boeing 757.

In addition to the engines, another key to the C-17's impressive performance is the installation of externally blown flaps. These were demonstrated and tested on the AMST YC-15 and shown to provide tremendous lift. The fixed-vane, double-slotted flaps are lowered behind the engine exhaust nozzles thereby deflecting the thrust downward and increasing lift on takeoff. Engine exhaust blown over the top of the flap also creates lift—the Coanda Effect—which decreases the airplane's takeoff roll and allows for a lower minimum controllable air speed, steeper descents onto shorter runways, and reduced landing roll. Using the blown-flap system and engine-thrust reversers which blow forward and up, a C-17 carrying more than 167,000 pounds of cargo can land in less than 3,000 feet.

On the inside, the cockpit seats a pilot and co-pilot operating the aircraft from state-of-the-art flight stations. Each has a full-time, all-function heads-up display (HUD) enabling him or her to read the primary flight parameters while looking through the windscreen. These units can be stowed when they are not needed or when using night vision goggles (NVGs). The instrument panel has four multi-function cathode-ray tube (CRT) displays with analog back-ups. These provide flight information and monitor various systems on the aircraft. The fly-by-wire control system is quad-redundant and has a mechanical back-up.

The cargo bay has loadmaster stations forward and aft, and the interior can be reconfigured in flight from all-cargo to passenger seating or a combination of both. Along the sidewalls are 54 permanently installed seats, 27 per side, and palletized seating can accommodate an additional

100. There are three aeromedical evacuation litter stations that accommodate three litters each on board, and nine more can be added, enabling 36 stretcher patients to be carried. Trucks and Humvees can be transported in two side-by-side rows, or three Bradley fighting vehicles along the centerline, or one M-1 main battle tank plus other smaller vehicles will fill a C-17.

Advanced composite materials make up 14,000 pounds of the C-17's empty weight, much

After arriving from Yokota AB, Japan, this C-17A has its full load of 18 pallets quickly off-loaded by members of the 60th Aerial Port Squadron at Travis AFB. Refueled and reloaded, a new crew will start on a return mission to Yokota less than three hours later. The original crew will then fly another C-17 home to Charleston AFB after a 36-hour crew rest period. *Jim Dunn*

Named for Lt. Gen. William H. Tunner, commander of the Berlin Airlift, the Tunner is the latest in aircraft cargo loaders. Capable of handling 60,000 pounds of cargo, the Tunner can rise from 39 inches to 18 feet 6 inches to line up with the cargo deck of any transport aircraft. A fully loaded C-17 can be off-loaded in about 45 minutes using two Tunners. *Jim Dunn*

of it used to make landing gear doors and flight control surfaces.

Delays in the C-17 program saw the Department of Defense announce that the production line would be closed after 40 planes were acquired unless the planes could be delivered on schedule, on cost, and with the quality expected. After the manufacturer addressed the military's concerns and offered the opportunity to cut costs with a multi-year purchase of 80 more aircraft, the additional planes were contracted on May 31, 1996. This action reduced procurement costs by $1 billion and enabled Boeing (which completed acquisition of McDonnell Douglas on August 4, 1997) to plan and procure materials for the C-17 in a more effective and efficient manner.

At a length of 174 feet and with a wingspan of 170 feet, the C-17A is only slightly larger than a C-141B. It is the width of the cargo compartment and maximum payload weight that is nearly double that of the Starlifter. Eventually, the C-17 will perform every type of mission now flown by the C-141, including those in special operations for which AMC has asked for 15 modified C-17As. *Jim Dunn*

Seeing the C-17 co-pilot's view of a KC-135 with refueling boom deployed, it's not hard to imagine the tense nature of an aerial refueling operation prior to hook-up, during refueling and separation. Flying two huge planes in such close proximity takes skill and nerve. *Greg L. Davis*

The savings brought the cost of a C-17 down from $338 million each to $173 million. The Air Force will acquire a fleet of 120 Globemaster IIIs. Peak production will reach 15 aircraft per year, and Boeing will deliver the 120th C-17 in 2004.

The first C-17 flew from Long Beach, in California, on September 15, 1991, with McDonnell Douglas pilot Bill Casey at the controls. The flight

test program lasted from September 1991 through December 1994, when the aircraft's operating envelope and flying characteristics were determined. These tests showed that the airplane could fly at 575 miles per hour, had a service ceiling of 41,000 feet, and a maximum gross weight of 585,000 pounds. Aerial refuelings were also conducted, as well as paratrooper deployments and

The conflict in Bosnia provided the first test for the C-17 in a large-scale airlift operation. Flights from the United States to various locations in Europe delivered personnel and equipment to support the deployment. Stopovers at former Warsaw Pact airfields, such as this one made by C-17A (94-0067) at Taszar, Hungary, are no longer unusual for USAF aircraft. *Greg L. Davis*

C-17s were designed to operate with the smallest number of flight crew of any large transport. Only a pilot, co-pilot, and loadmaster are needed under normal operating conditions. However, since many missions are of long duration or consist of extended periods overseas, the flight crew is often augmented with additional personnel. *Greg L. Davis*

airdrops of 60,000 pound cargo loads. Also during this period, 22 world records were set—14 in December 1992 and seven in October 1993 (including 133,422 pounds carried to 36,653 feet). Ten other payload records and three time-to-climb marks have since been set. One of the most impressive records was a payload to altitude/time-to-climb plus short take off and landing record where a C-17 lifted off in under 1,400 feet, flew its load to 44,000 feet, and then made a full-stop landing in less than 1,400 feet.

On May 29, 1997, the first C-17 of the multi-year buy began assembly at Long Beach when its wing spars were installed in production jigs. One year later, on May 21, 1998, the 40th C-17,

Table I—C-17 Globemaster III Specifications

Length:	174 feet, 0 inches
Wing Span:	170 feet, 0 inches
Height:	55 feet, 1 inch
Empty Weight:	227,000 pounds
Maximum Weight:	585,000 pounds
Maximum Payload:	170,400 pounds — up to 172,000 pounds
Maximum Cruising Speed:	0.77 Mach
Unrefueled Range with 130,000 pound Payload:	3,200 miles
Powerplants:	Four Pratt & Whitney F117PW-100 turbofans rated at 41,700 pounds thrust each
Crew:	Three (pilot, co-pilot, loadmaster)

A number of C-17s have been given names that salute the "Spirit" of the Air Force and its supporters. One of these aircraft is C-17A (96-0005) the *Spirit of Sgt. John L. Levitow*. For actions as a loadmaster on a severely damaged AC-47 over South Vietnam on February 24, 1969, Sgt. Levitow became the lowest ranking airman to be presented the Medal of Honor. *Jim Dunn*

The first appearance of a C-17 at the Airlift Rodeo came in 1994 when 90-0533 made several demonstration flights. In 1998, this aircraft returned as a competitor flown by the 97th AMW, which uses eight C-17s to train aircrew at Altus AFB, Oklahoma. Seen here departing on one of its 1998 Rodeo flights, the team from Altus defeated two teams from Charleston AFB to take the title of Best C-17 Wing. *Jim Dunn*

and last from the original contract, was delivered to the Air Force. This aircraft was christened *Spirit of the Total Force*. To build a C-17, parts from more than 1,000 suppliers employing 15,000 workers must come together at exactly the right time. Boeing employs more than 12,000 people to provide parts, sub-assemblies, and to construct the C-17.

In May 1995, the C-17 team—Air Force, McDonnell Douglas, and subcontractors—was awarded the Collier Trophy for aeronautical achievement during 1994. This group was selected by the National Aeronautical Association for "designing, developing, testing, producing, and placing into service the Globemaster III whose performance and efficiency make it the most versatile airlift aircraft in aviation history."

Remembering the contributions others have made to the Air Force over the years, it is naming each C-17 after a person, city, or theme that represents the spirit of the service. Serial number 96-0005 has been christened *Spirit of Sgt. John L. Levitow*. Levitow was awarded the Medal of Honor for his actions as loadmaster on a badly damaged AC-47 gunship over South Vietnam on February 24, 1969. He was the lowest ranking airman to be presented the Medal of Honor. Entertainer Bob Hope was also on hand to christen his namesake, C-17A *Spirit of Bob Hope*. The 93-year-old entertainer and his wife attended a ceremony at the Long Beach factory for the unveiling.

On January 17, 1995, the Air Force declared the initial operational capability (IOC) of the 17th Airlift Squadron of the 437th Airlift Wing,

Soon the sight of a C-17 coming or going from McChord AFB, Washington, will become a familiar one. In late 1999, the 62nd AW will receive its first C-17 on the way to becoming the second active duty Globemaster III wing. The first ANG unit to get C-17s will be the 172nd AW at Jackson, Mississippi, which will receive the final aircraft from the initial order of 120. *Jim Dunn*

Charleston Air Force Base, South Carolina. The squadron was operationally ready for deployment in support of American forces having 12 aircraft and 48 crews fully qualified. Two additional squadrons of the 437th, the 14th and 15th, as well as the 317th Airlift Squadron of the 315th Airlift Wing (Reserve), both based at Charleston, will receive a total of 48 C-17s. The 97th Air Mobility Wing, Altus Air Force Base, Oklahoma, began receiving the first of its eight aircraft in April 1996 for initial crew training on the type.

McChord Air Force Base, Washington's 62nd Airlift Wing and 446th Airlift Wing (Reserve) will receive the C-17 in July 1999. The 172nd Airlift Wing of the Mississippi Air National Guard stationed at Jackson will transition into six aircraft beginning in July 2004.

Operationally, the C-17 has supported numerous military and humanitarian aid efforts around the globe. During Operation Balkan Journey between December 1995 and February 1996, C-17s deployed U.S. forces to support NATO

On November 10, 1972, the U.S. Air Force contracted for two designs in its AMST (Advanced Medium STOL Transport) program. Boeing entered the YC-14 and McDonnell Douglas the YC-15, each company building two prototypes. These AMST designs demonstrated the concept of externally blown flaps that produce powered lift giving amazing short-field take off and landing performance. Many of the lessons learned on the YC-15 were incorporated into the C-17 design. *Michael Carter*

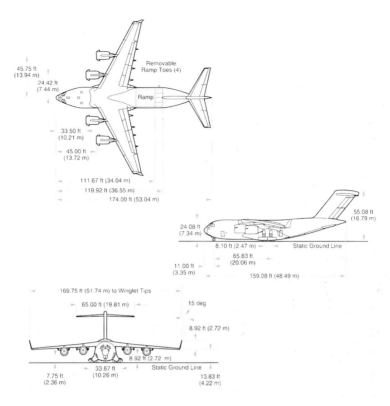

45.75 ft (13.94 m)
24.42 ft (7.44 m)
Removable Ramp Toes (4)
Ramp
33.50 ft (10.21 m)
45.00 ft (13.72 m)
111.67 ft (34.04 m)
119.92 ft (36.55 m)
174.00 ft (53.04 m)

55.08 ft (16.79 m)
24.08 ft (7.34 m)
8.10 ft (2.47 m)   Static Ground Line
65.83 ft (20.06 m)
11.00 ft (3.35 m)
159.08 ft (48.49 m)

169.75 ft (51.74 m) to Winglet Tips
65.00 ft (19.81 m)
15 deg
8.92 ft (2.72 m)
8.92 ft (2.72 m)   Static Ground Line
7.75 ft (2.36 m)
33.67 ft (10.26 m)
13.83 ft (4.22 m)

Loadmaster Station
85.17 ft (25.96 m) Double Row Loadable Length
Safety Aisle   Paratroop Doors   Ramp Toes
Crew Door
68.17 ft (20.78 m)
19.83 ft (6.04 m)

44.75 ft (13.64 m) (Ref.)
37.50 ft (11.43 m) (Ref.)
14.75 ft (4.50 m)
10.67 ft (3.25 m)
Cargo Door (Open Position)
Safety Aisle
12.33 ft (3.76 m)   13.50 ft (4.11 m)
Ramp Up 10 deg
10.50 ft (3.20 m)
5.33 ft (1.63 m) Floor Height
Static Ground Line
Ramp Down 9 deg
Ramp Toes Down 15 deg

General	
Wing Area	3800 ft^2/353 m^2
Wing Sweep	25 deg
Aspect Ratio	7.165
Cruise Speed	Mach 0.74-0.77
Max TOGW	585,000 lb/265,352 kg
Max Payload (2.25 g)	170,400 lb/77,292 kg
Usable Fuel Weight	181,054 lb/82,125 kg

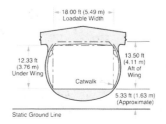

18.00 ft (5.49 m) Loadable Width
12.33 ft (3.76 m) Under Wing
13.50 ft (4.11 m) Aft of Wing
Catwalk
5.33 ft (1.63 m) (Approximate)
Static Ground Line

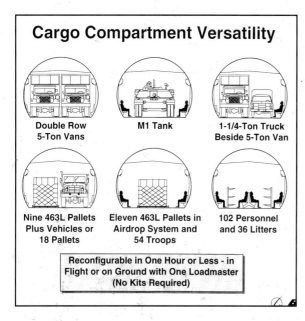

Cargo Compartment Versatility

Double Row 5-Ton Vans

M1 Tank

1-1/4-Ton Truck Beside 5-Ton Van

Nine 463L Pallets Plus Vehicles or 18 Pallets

Eleven 463L Pallets in Airdrop System and 54 Troops

102 Personnel and 36 Litters

Reconfigurable in One Hour or Less - in Flight or on Ground with One Loadmaster (No Kits Required)

These cargo compartment versatility diagrams show six different interior configurations that can be used for the Globemaster III. *Boeing*

Table II— C-17 Globemaster III Serial Numbers

Serial	Count
87-0025	(1)
88-0265/-0266	(2)
89-1189/-1192	(4)
90-0532/-0535	(4)
92-3291/-3294	(4)
93-0599/-0604	(6)
94-0065/-0070	(6)
95-0102/-0107	(6)
96-0001/-0008	(8)
97-0041/-0048	(8)
98-0049/-0057	(9)
99-0058/-0070	(13)
00-0071/-0085	(15)
01-0086/-0100	(15)
02-0101/-0115	(15)
03-0116/-0120	(5)

peacekeeping efforts in Tuzla, Bosnia, and flew humanitarian aid to Sarajevo. C-17s flew 27 percent of the U.S. airlift missions and delivered 57 percent of the total tonnage with a 98 percent departure reliability rating. During one C-17 delivery on December 8 at Sarajevo, French NATO troops unloaded 154,000 pounds of pressed wood and gas heaters in less than 35 minutes. When people are starving and cold, the C-17's load carrying capacity is extremely appreciated—a C-130 can deliver five pallets of supplies while the C-17 will supply 18.

On February 2, 1996, a C-17 supported by KC-10 Extender tankers flew nonstop from Travis Air Force Base, California, to Tuzla Air Base, Bosnia, to deliver 40 tons of fence posts to mark mine fields that litter the countryside. The trip took 14.5 hours.

Later that year, on November 26, C-17s deployed a Tanker Airlift Control Element (TALCE) to Entebbe, Uganda, to establish a hub in support of the multinational humanitarian aid airlift to central Africa. On March 24, 1997, C-17s brought planners to Libreville International Airport in the Republic of Gabon, in western Africa, to set up a possible evacuation of Americans from Zaire.

The longest airdrop in history was made on September 14, 1997 when twelve KC-135 Stratotankers and five KC-10s deployed to Moron Air Base, Spain, and refueled eight C-17 Globemaster IIIs flying airborne troops from North Carolina to Kazakhstan during CENTRAZBAT '97. The flight lasted almost 20 hours. CENTRAZBAT is a joint operation between the U.S. and forces from the former Soviet Union to provide training to enable Kazakhstan's military to participate in peacekeeping missions.

Certainly one of the most unusual loads carried by a C-17 was the October 28, 1997,

An AH-64 Apache attack helicopter is loaded aboard a C-17 at Hunter Army Airfield, Savannah, Georgia, on October 5, 1997. Eight C-17s were used to transport AH-64 helicopters as part of Bright Star '98, an extensive military exercise involving the U.S. Army, Air Force, Marine Corps, Navy, Air National Guard, and special operations forces from the United States and forces from Egypt, the United Arab Emirates, Kuwait, France, Italy, and the United Kingdom. *Boeing*

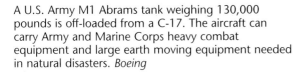

A U.S. Army M1 Abrams tank weighing 130,000 pounds is off-loaded from a C-17. The aircraft can carry Army and Marine Corps heavy combat equipment and large earth moving equipment needed in natural disasters. *Boeing*

A C-17 roars off the dirt strip at Barstow-Daggett, California, during a 30-day Air Force operation evaluating the aircraft's capabilities. Twelve C-17s from the 437th Airlift Wing at Charleston AFB, South Carolina, participated in the operation transporting Army and Air Force equipment and supplies from Charleston and Pope AFB, North Carolina, to and from the California airfield. Barstow-Daggett simulated a forward operating base that might be used in a wartime contingency operation. *Boeing*

shipment of a MiG-29B two-seat fighter from the Republic of Moldova to the United States. Both nations have an agreement to ensure that combat-capable equipment such as the MiG is not acquired by terrorist countries.

The C-17 will be the Air Force's core airlifter for the foreseeable future and has established itself as a prime player in the service's Global Reach-Global Power doctrine. In the future, will the C-17 undergo modifications in the same manner that the C-141 and C-5 did? Will we eventually see a stretched C-17? When the world's political situation changes and peacekeepers need to be deployed, or when natural disasters strike, the Globemaster III will be on the front lines providing security, food, and comfort to those in need.

U.S. Army paratroopers from Ft. Bragg, North Carolina, float toward their landing zone after jumping from a C-17 Globemaster III. *Boeing*

6 Giant Soviet Cargo Planes

uring its years of dominance as a super-power, Russia built a tremendous airlifter fleet to support its military machine and far-flung sphere of influence. During the mid-1950s, Russia's Antonov Design Bureau completed and flew its turboprop- powered An-10, an 84-seat passenger airliner with the NATO codename Cat. This aircraft evolved into the An-12, NATO code name Cub, that featured a tall tail and rear cargo-loading ramp. From the Cub evolved the Cock—Antonov's An-22 Antheus—which flew for the first time on February 27, 1965. The Antheus is powered by 15,000-horsepower NK-12MA engines driving eight-blade, constant-speed, con-trarotating propellers. Its wing span is 211 feet, 4 inches, the fuselage is 190 feet long, and the height over the tail is equal to a four-story build-ing at 41 feet, 1 inch. Its cargo compartment is 108 feet, 3 inches long and 14 feet, 5 inches in width and height, giving a cargo volume of more than 22,707 square feet. The An-22 can transport 176,400 pounds for 3,100 miles.

Designed to replace the An-12, Ilyushin pro-duced the Il-76T, NATO code name Candid-A (civil) or Candid-B (military). It was first flown in March 1971 and entered service three years later. This aircraft is operated by both the military and civilian air arms of the Russian Federation, and more than 850 of the type have been built. Its size puts the Il-76 in a class with Lockheed's C-141 Starlifter, having a 165-foot, 8-inch wing span, a 152-foot, 10.5-inch fuselage, and a maximum take

Here is proof that the Cold War is really over. A civilian An-124 sits on a former Strategic Air Command flightline after delivering Soviet moon rocket motors to an American company. This VolgaDnepr An-124, RA-82043, is seen at Mather Field near Sacramento, California, on August 30, 1996, after delivery of 12 NK-33 rocket motors. Next stop is Los Angeles to pick up equipment for a Michael Jackson concert in Czechoslovakia. VolgaDnepr/HeavyLift is a Russian-British joint venture. *Jim Dunn*

While the An-12 *Cub* is the Soviet equivalent of the Lockheed C-130, the An-22 is unlike any American military transport. First flown in February 1965 and in production until 1974, the An-22 has a military payload that was not surpassed until the introduction of the Lockheed C-5. Today about 40 of the aircraft remain in the inventory of the Russian air force.

Table I—An-124 Condor Specifications

Length:	226 feet, 8.5 inches
Wing Span:	240 feet, 5.75 inches
Height:	68 feet, 2 inches
Maximum Takeoff Weight:	892,872 pounds
Maximum Cruising Speed:	537 miles per hour
Maximum Range:	2,795 miles
Payload:	300,000 pounds
Powerplants:	Four 51,590 pound thrust Ivchenko Progress ZMKB Lotarev D-18T turbofan engines

off weight of 374,785 pounds. These pure-jet powered transports can carry a 96,000-pound payload for more than 3,100 miles. In a troop-carrying configuration, an Il-76 can deliver 140 fully equipped troops to remote airfields, or airdrop 125 paratroopers. Four Soloviev D-30KP turbofan engines producing 26,455 pounds of thrust enable the Il-76 to operate into and out of rough landing strips in Siberia, supporting military and governmental projects such as the construction of bridges, roads, factories, power generating plants, and mining expeditions. Export versions of the Il-78 were sold to Poland, Czechoslovakia, Iraq, and other countries allied with the Russian Federation.

Two aerial-refueling versions of the Il-76 are now in service. The Il-78 convertible tanker has removable 4,748-gallon tanks, while the Il-76M, exclusively employed in the tanker role, has the capacity of off-loading 6,105 gallons of fuel.

More than 14 years after Lockheed's C-5 first flew, the Antonov Design Bureau in Kiev rolled out its An-124. Given the NATO codename Condor, the aircraft first flew on December 26, 1982,

The Soviet emphasis on continued development of more powerful turboprop engines made this large transport possible. Each of the four Kuznetsov NK-12MA turboprops produce 15,000 horsepower, driving eight-blade, constant-speed, contrarotating propellers. Cruising speed is 373 mph, and with a 99,000-pound payload, the An-22 has a range of 6,805 miles. Of note on this aircraft is the row of chaff and flare dispensers on top of the main gear well. *Michael Gruenenfelder*

Looking like a veteran of the Afghanistan War, this An-22 Cock wears a seldom seen tactical paint scheme. Fitted with a rail-mounted, overhead traveling crane to ease cargo movement, the An-22 can carry a 176,400-pound payload in its 108-foot-long cargo compartment. The forward cabin is pressurized for the crew of five and up to 29 passengers. *Michael Gruenenfelder*

Looking more like a bomber than a transport, the Il-76 is one of the few transports ever designed with defensive armament. Il-76s that were built for the Soviet military had two 23-mm twin-barrel GSh-23L cannons fired by a gunner positioned in a tail-mounted turret much like a World War II B-17. This aircraft belongs to Transport Aviation, air force of the Russian Federation.

NATO gave the name Candid-A to the civil Il-76T variants and Candid-B to the Il-76M military variants. It was very common for a Soviet military transport to appear in the markings of Aeroflot, and this practice continues in the new Russian Federation. This Il-76M in Aeroflot markings has the new flag of the Russian Federation over the old flag of the Soviet Union.

becoming the largest cargo plane in the world—a title it would hold for less than six years. Similar in appearance to the C-5, the Condor also has an upward swinging nose door. Its wing span is 18 feet greater than the Galaxy, but its fuselage is 21 feet shorter. The plane boasts a 24-wheel main landing gear and two 2-wheel steerable nose gear enabling the An-124 to operate from unprepared strips and hard-packed snow. More than 12,000 pounds of composite structures were incorporated into its construction, shaving more than 4,000 pounds off of the Condor's total weight.

The 6,760-square-foot, 32- to 35-degree swept wing holds four underwing 51,590 pound thrust Lotarev D-18T turbofan engines, and features triple-slotted Fowler flaps, leading edge slats, spoilers, and large air brakes. Ten wing fuel tanks hold 507,063 pounds of avgas giving the An-124 a fully loaded range of 2,795 miles. The fuselage cargo hold is 118 feet, 1 inch long, 21

Ilyushin developed two tanker versions of the Candid to meet the growing need for air refueling within the Soviet air force. Named Midas by NATO, both versions feature three RAM air turbine-driven UPAZ-1A Sakhalin refueling pods. The Il-78 is the tanker/transport version with two removable 4,748-gallon tanks, while the Il-78M has three permanent 6,105-gallon tanks for its sole mission as a tanker. Here an Il-78M refuels a Tupolev 95 Bear maritime reconnaissance plane.

feet wide, and 14 feet, 5 inches tall, giving a total cargo volume of more than 35,900 cubic feet.

Antonov built 48 An-124s, of which 21 are operated by civilian companies such as Aeroflot, HeavyLift, and Volga Dnepr. These companies generate hard currency through the lease of these aircraft and by moving outsized commercial cargo to points throughout the world. Relief supplies, World Cup sailboats, commercial satellites, the Rockefeller Center Christmas tree, and even musician Michael Jackson's concert tour equipment have been carried by An-124s. They have also been used to transport sections of Airbus Industries' A330 and A340 widebody airliners between factories in the United Kingdom, Canada, and France.

In order to keep up with American technology, the Soviet Union needed to develop both airborne early warning and control system (AWACS) aircraft and airborne command and control (ABCC) posts. The Il-76 airframe was chosen to support these systems, with the Il-76MD being outfitted for the ABCC mission and the Beriev A-50 Mainstay becoming the AWACS plane, complete with large rotating radome. It is interesting to note that this A-50 is shown in Aeroflot markings.

A pair of Su-27 Flanker fighters provide escort for this An-124 Condor of the Voeynno-Transportnaya Aviatsiya (Transport Aviation), air forces of the Russian Federation. Of the 48 Condors built to date, 27 have been for military service, with 21 aircraft going into civilian service. So far, one military and three civilian An-124s have been lost in crashes.

The Soviets called it Mriya, the Ukrainian word for "dream," but the sole example of the An-225 is known as Cossack by NATO. It is now used rarely in its intended support mission for the Buran Space Shuttle and is, instead, often sent on flights to demonstrate the capabilities of the Ukrainian aircraft industry. Portions of a second An-225 have been built. *Michael Gruenenfelder*

When building the An-225, designers borrowed as much as possible from the An-124 Condor. Using the same type of engine as the Condor, the An-225 can carry a 551,000-pound payload either internally or on top of its fuselage. Maximum takeoff weight is 1,322,770 pounds, but that requires a runway length of more than 11,400 feet. Ground operations also are hindered by the absence of a rear cargo entry ramp. *Michael Gruenenfelder*

Developed directly from the An-124, Antonov's An-225 Mriya, NATO code name Cossack, is a six-engine airlifter that is now the world's largest aircraft and biggest cargo plane. Built at Kiev, Ukraine, it flew its maiden flight on December 21, 1988.

Table II— An-225 Mriya Specifications

Length:	275 feet, 7 inches
Wing Span:	290 feet
Maximum Takeoff Weight:	1,322,770 pounds
Maximum Cruising Speed:	530 miles per hour
Maximum Range:	2,795 miles
Powerplants:	Six 51,590 pound thrust Ivchenko Progress ZMKB Lotarev D-18T turbofan engines

The An-225 is nearly one and one-half times larger than the Condor. It has a redesigned twin-tail rather than the An-124's conventional tail, six 51,500-pound-thrust engines, and its wings are nearly 50 feet wider, spanning 290 feet. A new wing torsion box was built to handle larger aerodynamic loads on the An-225's wings. In the cockpit, the avionics and flight software are identical to the An-124's. To spread the giant loads carried by the An-225, four additional wheels were added to the main undercarriage bringing the total to 28, of which 20 are steerable.

The Mriya made its debut at the 1989 Paris Air Show with the Buran Space Shuttle carried externally between the wings. The aircraft never entered full-scale production. Two aircraft were constructed, of which only one ever flew and it was reported to be in storage at the end of 1998.

7 The Future of Airlifters

argo aircraft will undergo a tremendous transition during the next 20 years. The Air Force plans to eliminate the C-141 Starlifter from its inventory by 2006. Boeing C-17s that are being acquired today could be flying until the year 2040.

Other Air Force tanker/transports are also nearing the end of their useful lives. KC-135 tanker/transports which supplement larger cargo aircraft are expected to be eliminated by 2013. The larger McDonnell Douglas KC-10A Extender which refueled 25 percent of the aircraft during Operation Desert Storm, also moved 54 million pounds of cargo and 6,700 passengers. The multi-mission capabilities of these aircraft will be designed into America's future giant cargo planes.

Although the Air Force has plans to begin retiring the C-5 Galaxy in 2007, Lockheed-Martin Aeronautical Systems has teamed with General Electric Aircraft Engines and Honeywell Defense Avionics Systems to propose a C-5 modernization program. The trio of aerospace companies hopes to extend the life of existing C-5s to the year 2030—making it conceivable that many aircraft will be operational more than 50 years after their first flight.

Re-engining the C-5 fleet would also improve its reliability. The Air Force's San Antonio Air Logistics Center at Kelly Air Force Base, Texas, sponsored a study to improve the C-5's dispatch rates. They determined that by replacing the Galaxy's General Electric TF-39-1C engines with GE CF6-80C2L1F turbofans, the Galaxy's reliability rates would double. Structural modifications enabling C-5s to use the new engine package would be minimal. Current TF-39-1C engines used on the C-5 are expensive to maintain,

Artist's concept of the MD-17 in civilian colors. This short-field accessible, high-wing, four-engine, T-tailed freighter would be used to carry heavy and outsize commercial loads to destinations where port facilities and overland routes are unavailable. *Boeing*

whereas parts for commercial CF6-80 turbofans are readily available and, in comparison, relatively inexpensive. CF6-80 engines are flown on Boeing's 747 and 767, the Airbus A300, A310, and A330, as well as the Boeing/McDonnell Douglas MD-11. Airlines that fly the CF6-80 include Continental, Air New Zealand, LanChile, US Airways, and Delta Airlines. The military version of the CF6-80 engine, designated F103-GE-102, also powers Air Force One. A C-5 equipped with CF6-80 power plants is projected to have a 30 percent shorter takeoff roll and its time to cruising altitude with a full load would be reduced by 58 percent.

Other proposed improvements to the C-5 feature an avionics modernization program which will also use off-the-shelf commercial aircraft technology. Honeywell plans to offer its Versatile Integrated Avionics (VIA) system, which has been certified by the Federal Aviation Administration (FAA) for use on commercial aircraft. This new package includes Full Authority Digital Engine Control, liquid crystal flat-panel displays, and built-in upgrade capabilities.

Modernizing the C-5 fleet would reduce the cost per flying hour by 34 percent and the cost per ton-mile to transport cargo by 44 percent. The cost to achieve these reductions is only 20 percent of that required to purchase new aircraft. Lockheed-Martin puts the upgrade package cost at $35 million for each of the Air Force's more than 125 C-5s—76 C-5As and 50 C-5Bs. Both the C-5A and "B" models have a projected life of 30,000 airframe hours, and the C-5A fleet averages 16,000 hours while C-5Bs average 9,000 hours. A modernization program would be cost efficient and will keep the Galaxy in the Air Force's inventory for many years to come.

The economic situation in the former Soviet Union has virtually eliminated research and development budgets for large cargo aircraft. One new aircraft, the An-70, is being developed by the Antonov Design Bureau. In a size comparison, this new airlifter is between the Lockheed C-130 Hercules and C-141 Starlifter. It is powered by four 13,800-horsepower Progress D-27 turboprops that each turn two eight-blade, contra-rotating Stupino SV-27 propellers. The Russian and Ukrainian governments plan to jointly build 500 of the aircraft, 80 percent of which will go to the Moscow government. Unlike the Boeing C-17, which uses powered-lift devices, the An-70 relies on more conventional technology to enhance its Short Takeoff and Landing (STOL) characteristics. The An-70 is expected to lift a 55,115 pound payload from a 6,000-foot unimproved runway and deliver it to another unpaved strip more than 1,650 miles away.

Another tactical airlifter of the same size is under consideration in the United States. The Advanced Theater Transport (ATT) uses a tilt-wing assembly to supply super-short takeoff and landing (SSTOL) characteristics. This plane is planned to be similar in size to the C-130, yet it could operate from extremely small fields. Its landing speed is only 45 knots, allowing it to stop in only 750 feet. Concepts from Boeing (McDonnell Douglas) show a four-engine turboprop featuring a wing that pivots upwards at the rear wing spar. If Air Force funding becomes available for the project, flying prototypes could be tested around 2010.

Commercially, Boeing is making great efforts to adapt its versatile C-17 to the civil market as the MD-17. By eliminating the military-exclusive equipment, Boeing is hoping to provide a replacement for the fleet of aging commercial An-124s. Civilian An-124 operators have demonstrated that there is a market for a large cargo aircraft that can lift heavy, outsize cargo. Companies engaged in oil and mineral exploration, telecommunications, construction, space and satellite technology, and aerospace all use out-sized, heavy-lift aircraft to transport their products and equipment.

Using an MD-17, air freight forwarders would be able to deliver payloads to remote locations where cargo now has to be delivered to a seaport by ship, then trucked overland. This is an extremely important consideration when valuable loads must be trans-shipped to distant sites in under-developed nations where roads are often impassable or nonexistent. For example, as the expansion of power generation stations increases in areas such as China and South America, a manufacturer could deliver generators or construction equipment directly to the job site using an MD-17. Reduced delivery time for these goods means the project will be completed sooner, and it will be up and running, generating capital sooner, thereby increasing profits. To deliver a power generator from a seaport to a remote job site entails the construction of a road capable of supporting heavy loads. MD-17s would eliminate the need to undertake such mammoth support projects.

Without taking away any business from those companies already operating An-124s commercially, the market for a civil MD-17 fleet is estimated to be $8 billion by the year 2008. The MD-17's greatest advantage will be its reliability as well as its ability to operate into air fields where landing the An-124 is not feasible.

In the distant future, aerodynamic visionaries foresee tailless aircraft with joined-wings capable of airlifting troops and cargo while using two refueling probes to simultaneously tank-up a pair of receiving aircraft. Elimination of the tail reduces the plane's cross section and thereby its radar return, bringing stealth to the transport aircraft arena. These futuristic transports will have unrefueled global range, enabling them to depart bases in the United States and deliver men and materiel anywhere in the world. It is possible that future airlifters may not only refuel other aircraft, deploy paratroopers, and deliver cargo, but they may carry offensive weapons such as hypersonic cruise missiles.

This digitally enhanced photo of a military C-17 off-loading NASA cargo represents what a civilian MD-17 would look like in action. Commercial importers/exporters sending cargo by ship is the prime market for the MD-17. Of the material carried by ship, it is estimated that the market share for heavy-lift aircraft would amount to 2.4 million tons annually. *Boeing*

Military airlift and the concepts that determine the cargo planes of the future will undergo a radical change in the next 15 to 20 years. If power plant technology continues to evolve at today's tremendous rates, the possibilities for future airlifters are unlimited.

Index

Aircraft
    A-50 Mainstay (Beriev), 88
    AC-130H Spectre gunship (Lockheed), 18
    An-10 Cat (Antonov Design Bureau), 83
    An-12 Cub (Antonov Design Bureau), 83, 84
    An-22 Cock (Antonov Design Bureau), 83–85
    An-70 (Antonov Design Bureau), 94
    An-124 Condor (Antonov Design Bureau), 83, 85, 86, 88, 89
    An-225 Cossack (Antonov Design Bureau), 90, 91
    Ar-232 (Arado), 13
    B-17 Flying Fortress, 11
    B-24 Liberator, 11
    C-5 Galaxy (Lockheed), 29, 36–49, 93, 94
    C-17 Globemaster III, 64–81, 93, 94
    C-46 Commando (Curtiss), 14
    C-47 Skytrain (Douglas), 9, 11, 14, 16
    C-54 Skymaster (Douglas), 10, 14
    C-74 Globemaster I (Douglas), 15
    C-82 Packet (Fairchild), 14
    C-97 Stratocruiser (Boeing), 15, 17
    C-118A (Douglas), 11
    C-119 Flying Boxcar (Fairchild), 15, 16
    C-124 Globemaster II (Douglas), 13, 16
    C-130 Hercules (Lockheed), 14, 17–19, 29, 30
    C-133 Cargomaster (Douglas), 17
    C-135 Stratolifter (Boeing), 17
    C-141 Starlifter (Lockheed), 20–35, 93
    Constellation (Lockheed), 15
    DC-2 (Douglas), 11
    DC-4E (Douglas), 11
    DC-10-30CF (McDonnell Douglas), 51, 52
    Ford Tri-Motor, 9
    Fw-200 Condor (Focke-Wulf), 13
    Il-76 (Ilyushin), 83, 85, 86
    Il-78M (Ilyushin), 87
    Ju-52 (Junkers), 11
    Ju-52/3 (Junkers), 11, 13
    KC-10A Extender (McDonnell Douglas), 29, 50–63, 93
    KC-135 Stratotanker (Boeing), 17, 19, 29, 30, 93
    M-130 (Martin), 11
    MD-11 (Boeing/McDonnell Douglas), 94
    MD-17 (Boeing), 93–95
    Me-321 (Messerschmitt), 13
    Me-323 (Messerschmitt), 13
    XC-99 (Convair), 15
Boeing, 10, 38, 51, 65, 70
Bright Star '98, 79
Bush, President George, 35
CENTRAZBAT '97, 78

Clark, General Mark, 14
Cold War, 15, 16
Collier Trophy, 74
D-Day invasion, 14
Desert Storm, 35, 49, 59, 60
Douglas Company, The, 10, 38
General Electric, 38
General William G. Moore Jr. trophy, 29, 31
Kuiper Flying Observatory, 22
Lockheed, 10, 22, 38
Loughead, Allan, 10
Loughead, Malcolm, 10
Marrott, Major James E., 27
McDonnell Douglas, 51, 65, 67
Military Air Transport Service (MATS), 21, 22, 37
Military Airlift Command (MAC), 26, 28
NASA, 22
National Aeronautical Association, 74
Operation Babylift, 27, 45
Operation Balkan Journey, 76
Operation Blue Light, 25
Operation Countdown, 26
Operation Deep Freeze, 35
Operation Desert Shield, 26, 35, 49, 59, 60
Operation Dragoon, 14
Operation Eagle Thrust, 26
Operation El Dorado Canyon, 55, 57
Operation Enhance Plus, 43
Operation Homecoming, 27
Operation Just Cause, 25, 32, 33, 59
Operation Market-Garden, 14
Operation Nickel Grass, 27, 38, 43
Operation Restore Hope, 49
Operation Slapstick, 14
Operation Urgent Fury, 25, 32
Operation Varsity, 14
Operation Weserübung, 13
Roosevelt, President Franklin D., 10
Sacred Cow, 10
Shinoskie, John J., 27
Spanish Civil War, 11
Spirit of Bob Hope, 67, 74
Spirit of Sgt. John L. Levitow, 73, 74
Spirit of the Total Force, 74
Vietnam, 25, 26, 42, 43
Volant Rodeo, 28–31
Volant Wind, 35
World War II, 9, 11, 13, 14
Yom Kippur War, 38, 43